Summerlands

A Personal Journey around the Underworld of the Glastonbury Zodiac

Jenny Chapman

Copyright

ISBN 978-0-9956188-4-8

Author's note

This book is based on the author's lived experience between the total solar eclipses of 21st August 2017 in Leo and 2nd July 2019 in Cancer, as well as journeys through the nine worlds of the Norse world tree, a one-year circuit of the Glastonbury zodiac and associated locations, and oral and published stories, myths and legends.

Contents

Foreword

Katherine Maltwood (1878 – 1961) is credited with discovering the Giant effigies forming the Glastonbury Zodiac. Thought to have been carved out over 4,000 years ago and to be formed by the rivers, hills and ancient roads in the Somerset landscape, they are depicted within a 30-mile radius of Glastonbury with Park Wood at its centre. The zodiac contains astrological representations for: Aries (a lamb), Taurus (a bull), Gemini (a Christ child), Cancer (a ship), Leo (a lion), Virgo (the Goddess), Libra (a dove), Scorpio (a scorpion), Sagittarius (the sun king), Capricorn (a Unicorn), Aquarius (a Phoenix) and Pisces (two fish and a whale) along with the *Girt Dog of Langport*.

The zodiac or star temple represents a Garden of Eden or Paradise on Earth. Its magical function is in accordance with the principles 'like attracts like' and 'as above so below'. This is symbolised by the secret codes of sacred geometry built into each of its sites and religious buildings which are also shared with Plato's Ideal Republic and the ground-plans of Stonehenge. Glastonbury itself and the sacred sites in the surrounding landscape represent a cosmo-magical centre. Via a system of labyrinths and underground watercourses, tunnels and chambers (along with the straight alignments of Ley lines) the Earth's living energies are used to fuse cosmic and terrestrial forces. In this way, the power to influence human affairs is harnessed.

Mystical alignments such as the Melkarth and Maltwood's Equinox Line connect key geographic points and sacred structures across the landscape. These include: the Temple of Hercules and the Nymph Grotto at Stourhead; King Alfred's Tower; Bruton, Hornblotton, Street and Butleigh Churches; Cadbury Castle; St Joseph's Chapel at Glastonbury Abbey; Peak of Glastonbury Tor; Burrow Mump; Cheddar Gorge tumulus; Wells Cathedral and Ponter's Ball earthworks.

England

Glastonbury

For darling Kevin
A man who wanted everyone to be able to feel

Map of the Summer Lands

My route

Start: Langport (*Girt Dog of Langport*)

Journey through the astrological signs: Somerton (Leo); Babcary, Castle Cary and Ansford (Virgo); Barton St David and Park Wood (Libra); Hornblotten (Scorpio); West Pennard (Sagittarius); Ponter's Ball (Capricorn); Glastonbury Tor (Aquarius); the Holy Thorn (Pisces); Street and Walton Hill (Aries); Butleigh Monument (Taurus); Compton Dundon (Gemini); and lastly Liver Moor (Cancer).

Finish: Burrow Mump

Introduction

David, a local cunning man, and I, set off on our circular tour through the Glastonbury zodiac effigies on the day of a total solar eclipse in Leo. It was 21st August 2017. At that time, I didn't realise eclipses are the time for shadow work and setting new patterns. Nor did I understand that my return to Somerton, on the Zodiac's lion-paw and the place of my birth, would eventually help me to integrate major life-lessons and allow a unique self-expression to surface. I was only truly to know this when I stood once more on Brockle hill, in Somerton on 2nd July 2019.

Maybe it was a strange thing to do – to travel through the Glastonbury Zodiac as King Arthur's knights are said to have done – but back then it was my preference. I wanted to explore my local landscape, to find where Wagg Lane and Paradise lay on the *Girt Dog of Langport*, and to enter through its ancient portal on the day of a swirling bore. To feel the potent energies, on the shadowy edges of what was once a vast inland sea – the Virgoan witch's skirts, the old Dundon Fort on Gemini, the watery sea moors of Cancer – and to stand on Burrow Mump where the mysteries of sovereignty lay close by.

I didn't mind if the Zodiac mysteries were true or not. I was largely unconcerned with which historical period they belonged to and if the ancient Greeks built their mythology on that of the Sumerian astrologers in 2700 BC. It was Arthur's Round Table and the initiate's circuit which fired my imagination. I was after answers. What is life all about? Why do we attract different energetic patterns – people, experiences, luck – as we move through life to old age? What do our partners tell us about our own fears and abilities? Most of all, how can we heal and become more balanced? How does that magic really happen? By the end of my journey, I had learned some of the answers to those questions – about the influence of the planets, reincarnation and the evolving nature of consciousness.

David and I completed our circuit around the zodiac in Cancer, on the third Grand Trine in Water on July 9th, 2018. That Trine between Venus, Jupiter and Neptune forecast that doorways to past ways would be slammed shut, with the arrival of new desires, unexpected twists and unusual commitments. By then, some doors had already shut, and I had been deeply touched by others' lives and deaths. It was at my brother's remembrance service in late June 2018 that I saw through a labyrinth of deception which had been cast over the family many years earlier. It was as if a veil were lifted to reveal a dark spider's web. For a moment, I saw the world clearly.

Within months, my world shook again and quaked at its core, with the death of my partner. Consequently, I became interested by stories of the *Divine* or *Faery Marriage*. This involves a merging of human and ancestor intelligence into a symbiotic relationship that heals the fractured nature and ancestral DNA of both beings. Some say this marriage is connected to an ancient alliance between two species – human and Fae (a race called *Tuatha Dé Danann*) – which enables a bridge to be built across different levels of consciousness, for guidance and healing.

That year my aunt, and mother's twin sister, and a dear friend living in Australia also passed. In all, my family suffered ten miseries – deaths, life-changing accidents and illnesses – in just over a year. Through wide reading, I began to understand that our grief helps a loved one to complete the death process and travel to the realm of the dead. After this grieving is complete, new life can emerge.

My journey was not straightforward. Lessons came, concerning trauma, grief and identity. Yet, past problems continued to haunt me. It may have been a time conducive to difficult planetary aspects – between Pluto, my natal moon, Mercury and Venus. Certainly, I was the right age to experience a second Saturn return. Whether you believe peak experiences manifest when the planets are in certain relationships with each other or not, the scene was set to resolve old negative energies, stories and instinctive responses to environmental influences.

Many people – loved ones, family, teachers, therapists and friends – came forward to help. I tried their methods, but it was really the antidote to my fears which was needed, feeling through experience – engaging and exploring with people and in places that held the memories – my homelands.

The great mythologist Joseph Campbell states the first leg of the journey involves stages such as *The Call to Adventure, Refusal of the Call* and *Supernatural Aid*. Then we cross into *The Belly of the Whale*, the realm of night or the underworld. Here we often meet re-occurring mythological themes such as the *rebirth* and *dragons* and begin to use a symbolic language – dwarves, animals and birds – to describe our dilemma. These help us to translate challenges on an individual level.

Multiple journeys to *Yggdrasil*, the Norse world tree, helped my psyche develop out of its childhood stickiness and being 'trapped'. With guidance from a rune master, I visited the nine different realms of consciousness to understand their symbolic messages and lessons. Cranio-sacral therapy helped my body release the constrictions in my central nervous system. In time, layer upon layer of fear, wrong thinking and patterning came away. Meanwhile, setting foot on locations across the Zodiac and at places such as Wells Cathedral, Wookey Hole caves and the White Spring, along with tuition in the magical arts, opened my senses to a deeper way of feeling earth energy.

It wasn't merely the elements of these teaching methods which helped me – story, rhythm, play, energy transmission – it was the practitioners themselves. Their kindness and professional approach, certainly. Yet there was something more. Having completed their own personal journey, each understood the deep fears and challenges that lay ahead. They knew that with every shift in my psyche a corresponding change would arrive in my life, in the physical world. They helped cushion this impact by meticulous research into the 'right' timing for sessions, the apt choice of venue, careful tailoring of content to the fears I was likely to meet (both in the session and in the wider world) as well as gentle but humorous interpretation of my symbolic language for expressing those fears when they arose.

Story, myth and legend also helped. I read across different ages and mythologies. Many story images resonated with me on some deep level – family antiques floating down the river, how the Miller's daughter's story reflected the movements of Saturn and the *red-hot shoes*. However, it was mostly Arthurian stories which demonstrated a return to our true nature, and which I chose to include. They gave me a map to navigate the journey, one stamped into Somerset's race memory – our own creation story.

In the end, the zodiac's lessons neither came in the usual astrological order – Leo, Virgo, Libra, Sagittarius... – nor in one cycle. Instead I embodied their energies in a random order – Cancer, Pisces, Scorpio, Aries... – and needed to travel through parts of the zodiac several times. It was as if the alchemy of the astrological signs and their associated planets were contained in a spiral.

This spiral's completion coincided with the solar eclipse in July 2019. It was then my world began to take on a different shape and vibration. I was to realise how much my psyche had changed, and that I had eventually managed to get back in touch with the feelings in my body. The fears of my childhood had unraveled, each 'shade' stripped down to reveal another person underneath. In many ways, a more authentic sense of self emerged: one not so constricted by old trauma and ancestral patterns. One not always wanting to fly away.

In late August / early September of that year, the Grand Trine in Virgo affected the twelfth house in my astrological chart – the house of prisons, asylums, enemies, secrets and animals large enough to ride. A searing white light behind my eyes indicated the pineal gland or 3rd eye was clearing. Simultaneously, a series of short re-enactments of all-too-familiar past scenarios allowed me to clearly see what belonged to me and what belonged to others – and to release a continual cycle of shame, bullying and feelings of being unheard. Difficult people from my past came into sharp relief. For once I was able to face my fears head on – to experience a visceral reaction. With that came an ability to make decisions and execute my own plans. I started doing things for myself rather than relying on other people and gave up my addictions to food and tobacco, whilst others swore off alcohol. It was like I had been let out of a dark prison.

On 17th September, the planet Saturn completed its retrograde cycle and started going forward. My world began to change as new people and opportunities presented themselves. With this came an increasing sense of freedom and clarity. A joy at being able to participate in life and not flee to the other side – a lightness of being and a deep contentment around living my own life.

Afterwards, it seemed to me as if time itself – the circular movements of the planets and the cosmos – had dictated the course of my journey and the lifting of that dark spider's web.

'This being human is a guest house. Every morning a new arrival. A joy, a depression, a meanness, some momentary awareness comes as an unexpected visitor... Welcome and entertain them all. Treat each guest honorably. The dark thought, the shame, the malice, meet them at the door laughing, and invite them in. Be grateful for whoever comes, because each has been sent as a guide from beyond.'
Rumi

'If the doors of perception were cleansed every thing would appear to man as it is, infinite.'
William Blake

'O You who in a little boat, desirous to listen, have been following my craft which singing passes on, turn to see again your shores; put not out upon the deep; for haply, losing me, you would remain astray. The water which I take was never crossed. Minerva breathes, Apollo guides me, and the Muses nine point out to me the Bears.'
Dante's Divine Comedy

'I am Yesterday, Today, and Tomorrow, and I have the power to be born a second time. I am the divine hidden Soul who created the gods and gives sepulchral meals to the denizens of the deep, the places of the dead, and heaven... Hail, lord of the shrine that stands in the center of the earth. He is I, and I am he!'
Egyptian Book of the Dead

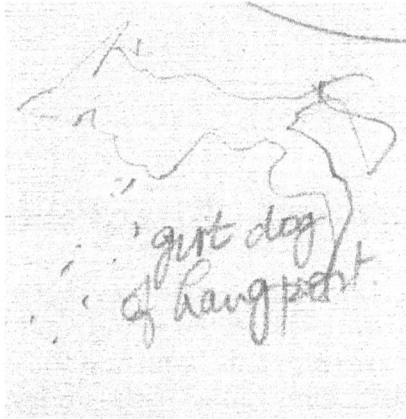

Each planet (and corresponding effigy on the zodiac) is linked to the Ladder of the Wise. This is a spiral process starting with calcification in Saturn (Capricorn, Aquarius), moving through dissolution in Jupiter (Sagittarius, Pisces), separation in Mars (Aries, Scorpio), conjunction in Venus (Taurus, Libra), fermentation in Mercury (Gemini, Virgo), distillation in the Moon (Cancer) and finally ending with coagulation in the Sun (Leo). The major events and landmarks in our lives provide the right time and necessary conditions for this alchemical transformation.

Associated places: Athelney, Burrow Mump, Aller, Oath hill, Langport, Wagg, Paradise

River Parrett, Langport

Chapter 1 - River Parrett

So I found myself at a turning point. The birds were mute, as if someone had simply switched off the sound, and I couldn't see much through the fog that enveloped the land and filled the valleys before me. An insistent pulse – beneath my nails, my eyelids, below the band of my old tracksuit bottoms – meant for once I was very much present, very much here.

The old man might always have been here. He was attuned to the landscape, this specific place in Somerset where Joseph of Arimethea planted his famous flowering staff, the Holy Thorn, and preached to the first-century king Arviragus.

His dress was unlikely – black motorcycle leathers and a bright red t-shirt. He just seemed to pop up before me, through a parting in the mist's curtain. If he acknowledged me, it wasn't through any deliberate effort. Nevertheless, he knew I was there. Yet his presence wasn't an imposition. I didn't feel self-conscious, as I usually did around people. Maybe it was being outdoors. Or maybe it was the silence.

I had come down to the river Parrett to get away from my cottage. Lately, my house didn't seem *me*. The lined bookshelves, the homely kitchen, it all seemed to meet somebody else's aspirations. Angela might sit in the armchair with her gold charm bracelet and sapphire ring as we shared gins and tonic, but I couldn't tell her about my feelings. Most likely, she would have brought the conversation back to sales figures and business targets. People don't warm to talk about bereavement or how a veil can lift to reveal a different reality to any known before. So I came down here, and though I wouldn't call it meditation exactly, I found a little perspective away from those four walls.

This week, my department had gone out for one of its intermittent drink-ups. I looked the part in my spaghetti-strap top and red high heels. No one could ever divine my feelings from a glance at my face. Yet I had gone with Graham, our new recruit, as much out of boredom as anything. There was something magnetic about him. He exuded a gentlemanly charm. Yet he was holding something back, at least from me.

When I looked around, the elderly man was revolving a ring on a weathered piece of string above a map. He didn't look so different from the caravan of travellers and fortune diviners who made their way across the sea moors. Some round here treated Somerset as if its sacred landscape were an initiatory circuit. A gateway to the unseen. They believed this was the garden from where the knights of *King Arthur* had set out on their quest for the Holy Grail, seeking to renew the blighted land. Within a thirty-mile radius of Glastonbury Tor, the landscape held, in no particular order: a paschal lamb, the Bull of Dawn, a dove, three bars of light, a scorpion, a Christ-head, Arthur's glass ship, Taliesin's Leo, the Triple Goddess, Arthur, Osiris, Chiron, a unicorn horn, a phoenix, two fish and a whale. People walked the Glastonbury circuit as if tracing Arthur's Round Table, treading a mirror of the constellations above them. In that respect, it was an English version of the pyramids.

The homemade pendulum swung back and forth over Nyland, Marchey, Panborough, Godney, Meare, Beckery – only to circle madly above the Isle of Avalon. 'The zodiac's lessons don't necessarily occur in a predictable fashion,' the man said. 'Life doesn't happen in straight lines.'

I didn't go over to him, but continued to listen as he told me a story.

'Fionnuala and her three younger brothers watched as their step-mother Aife raised her arms. As her cloak billowed, her thin fingers seemed to write on the wind:

'Be gone!' she called into the nothingness. 'No more!'

The old days, when the children could run with the swiftness of hares and swim with the grace of otters, sank into the mist. Times spent lying in the shade of a willow, peacefully watching the world float by, slipped their hold.

'An end!' Aife called, and their father's love – greater even than that for Aife herself – evaporated like dew on the wind.

'Enough!' and their mother's promise to watch over them in their dreams and when the greatest dangers came, all but vanished.'

He spoke in a way that suggested this might be a long tale.

'It was when their mother entered her long sleep that the first changes had come. Their father's smile, so quick among the halls, so bright upon the lake, retired below haunted eyes. His laugh faltered and went out. The beam that was his old self died. And then he met Aife, his wife's sister, and joy was restored. Yet Aife's cold angry heart would bear bitter fruit.

'A year after they last saw their mother, Aife invited the children to join her for an outdoor feast. Uneasy of step were the four as they waded into the lake before the picnic spot. The water-birds kept to their banks, and there were no calls from the surrounding canopies. Even the frogs and insects fell silent.

'I transform you into four swans! Their shapes will you retain for nine hundred years – three hundred on *Loch Dairbhreach*; three hundred on *Sruth na Maoilé*; and three hundred at *Iorrus Domnann and Inis Gluairé!*' Her cloak fell as she lowered her arms and resumed her human station.

'We will be revenged for such an action!' cried Fionnuala, and by speaking in just this fashion, she earned them the power of speech to allay the loneliness of the harsh centuries of trial to come. Whether through Fionnuala's words or not, Aife's actions cast her from the King's favour.

'So it was that for three-hundred years the children lived on the lake. After this time, their father's people no longer endured. 'No barks come from their dogs, nor smoke from their fires,' their father told them. 'Now, I too will sleep in the *Tír fo Thuinn*. But do not fear, I will come again.'

'When it was time to seek new lands, they bid farewell to the gentle deer, the playful otters and hares, and flew north, seeing how their father's lands had changed over three centuries. The fields lay derelict and overgrown. Untended, the lands ran to ruin. It was a depressing sight. Dispirited and seeking shelter before an advancing storm, they touched down in the lee of a cliff. Jellyfish, sea gooseberries and brittle stars; turtles, fan-worms and seals – the world and its creatures, as the children recognized them, had been transformed.

'In the early morning gloom, the four found a barren outcrop of rock from where they weathered a relentless storm. In future, they would return to this place of safety and should they ever become separated, their mother would see them straight. Her words were gentle and direct, marked by a luminescence promising safe passage and ports of call. Over the centuries, the children sang the songs of their people, and even taught the whale its beautiful song.

'One day, they awoke to realise the second part of their enchantment was over. Taking to the air, they journeyed south over mountainous bog and fields of scarlet pimpernel till they came upon a sheltered lake. There they made their home.

'In time, an old man wearing a grey cloak came and built himself a hut beside the lake. When he drifted asleep, the children took to aiding him with his handiwork. Before long, word spread and people from far and wide brought swords, shields and arrow tips to be remade by this new blacksmith and cast into a bell.

'One day, kneeling at the water's edge, he apologized for not having enough food to give to the swans. Fionnuala and her brothers replied that it was not necessary to demonstrate his true and gentle heart, for his actions spoke more eloquently than his words might ever intend. The blacksmith was dumbfounded. 'It is told of swans possessed of voices. The children of Lir, a magical race, long-disappeared!'

'After a further three-hundred years, a warrior came to consult the old man. He was the King of Connacht and had got wind of these mystical birds which spoke in human voices. As the children were captured and carried away, a bell began to toll. Mist swept over the lands and as it dispersed the children were revealed to be standing in place of the swans: aged, fleshless and close to death.

'Since then, much in this world has changed quickly. Yet not always will these past generations, the *Tuatha Dé Danann*, sleep.'

I came back to myself. The storyteller had not moved. I could still see his black leathers and red t-shirt out the corner of my eye. But there was a keenness to the air, and distant singing.

'On the zodiac, this area is the *Girt Dog of Langport*. The river draws the beast's jaw, throat and belly, Moon Drove is at his mouth and his tongue is the River Tone. It is the zodiac's western gateway, activated by a tidal bore swirling up the Severn and into the Parrett at Bridgwater. It is here we will start your journey through places which will nurture and bring you to maturity and reset your thinking patterns and relationships.'

He took a gnarled pencil and drew a circle filled with shapes. 'The lion, little dove, whale and ship will become important to you.'

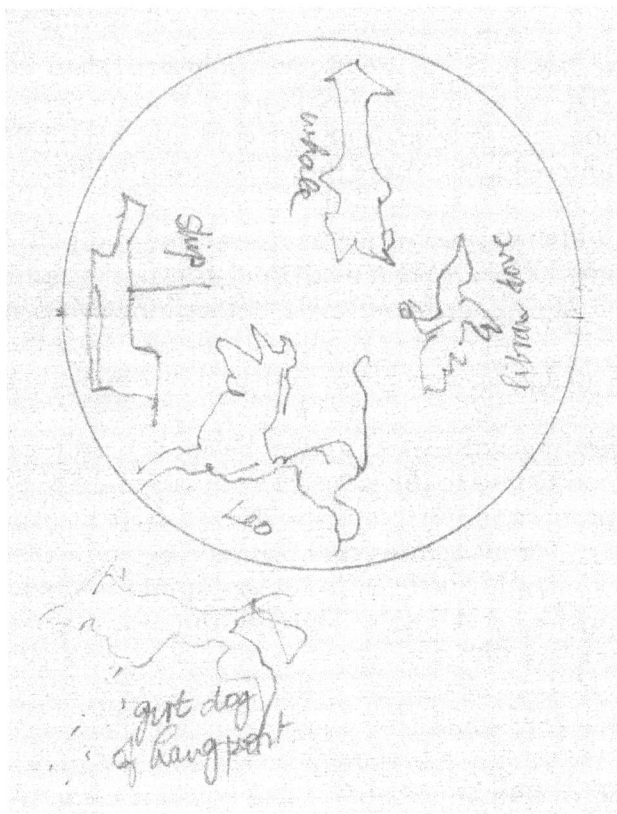

Tapping the circle, he continued. 'Arthur's Round Table represents the psyche; the Quest for the Holy Grail is an initiation journey or symbol of inner transformation. When mortally-wounded, Arthur is carried to the Isle of Avalon – the Celtic Isle of the Dead – where his soul journeys into the underworld. You are about to be initiated into the mysteries of death.'

Leo, July 24th – August 23rd

Leo symbolises creativity in the form of a coiled serpent. This sign represents the ego or where a person has most purpose in life.

Leo is associated with the Sun and the fifth house. The Sun is the Life Force. Through man's interaction with the world he becomes conscious of himself and evolves. The fifth house is where we express the inner part of ourselves that gives us pleasure and satisfaction. It represents productivity and sex outside of marriage.

Associated places: Somerton, Charlton Adam, Hurcot, Maggoty Paggoty, Copley Woods

Buttercross
Somerton

Chapter Two – Buttercross, Somerton

We met again, in a small town where some still speak the Old Language and communicate with the stones and the land itself. This town, situated on Leo's paw, was the place of my birth. Near-by, on the lion's tail, a carved devil adorned one of the church pew heads. The river Cary scratched its back. To my mind, this land was literally enchanted.

Some say the Lion begins the Zodiac, just as the slaying of the Nemean Lion began Hercules' famous labours. Others claim it represents sovereignty and the final rung of the spiritual process, the Sun beaming down on a child.

We made a circular walk around the octagonal pillars of the Buttercross, built for market traders in the 17th century. 'Eight is the number of magic. It means 'the ascended one' or 'the 13th dimension' and symbolizes a rebirth.'

From here, we headed out towards the old quarry at Catash. As we walked, he spoke of Somerton's history. 'It gives its name to Somerset or the Summerlands – a euphemism for the underworld. Once, its metal miners worked a secret resource deep underground. Deep below the town's protective escarpment, the river runs through a rich alluvial valley. As an ancient fortress, Somerton was variously the residence of West Saxon kings, the jail of King John of France and the target of the Danes' rampaging anger.'

The old man leaned into me as if he had something important to impart. 'In the legends, King Arthur's knights included his foster brother Sir Kay, his treacherous son Sir Mordred, the arrogant Sir Bleoberis who later became a hermit, Sir Lancelot and his son Sir Galahad, the Saracen knight Sir Palomides, Sir Ector de Maris the ladies' man and Sir Parzival and Sir Gawain famed for fighting the Red and Green knights. Other knights were known separately for their loyalty, cup-bearing duties and role as the court jester. However, at times, some of the knights of Arthur's Round Table – or the parts of his psyche – became unruly.'

He took a step back. 'Sir Lancelot, or Leo on the zodiac, was a personification of masculinity unable to learn from the feminine. Social status, duty and the subjugation of others became his sole aims. As one of Arthur's most trusted knights, this position changed when he fell in love with Arthur's wife, Queen Guinevere.'

Leo was the first time I looked into the heart of the storyteller. Really looked. That hot summer's day he was regal. His dress reminded me of a king on a hunt, attuned to the birds, animals and direction of the wind. He was a man at home in his environment.

'The spirits of the land are different wherever you go. Here they embody the gemstone Cassiterite, which helps release cellular memories and past life issues. It enables transference through inter-dimensional doorways and communication with other worlds.'

The storyteller stopped abruptly to pick up a flat, white stone. 'The ancestors speak through them,' he said. 'If you know how to talk to the stones, or the land and water, they can reveal the memories and wisdom of ancient forgotten races.'

A curry night with Graham came to me. 'Hello darling', he whispered at the gate. As we walked the garden path, I leant down to pick up a mysterious stone. 'Don't touch that', he said, but I did. We wandered into the house and its warming smell of spices, to the sweet sound of Abba's music. Graham was a mystic, I realised. He worked with the stone people – understood their messages and ability to carry energies.

'The human body produces a polarity similar to that along the major axes of crystals. In the electromagnetic field, like attracts like. Each bird has a different song and vibration, each plant and animal. We are attracted to those we need.'

The storyteller's voice continued in my inner ear.

'The king of the moles reclined on his throne, deep in the loamy Somerset levels. Vast clawed hands covered the pointed nose on his face, as he sat deep in thought. The young master had experienced numerous difficulties since the old lord, his father, had passed away. All day, things had been stirring in the young master's estate.

'When night fell, the king took the tunnel towards the gardens and the sight that awaited him stole his breath. Where for three hundred years a forest of magnificent oak trees had stood, he now witnessed a flattened plain.

'This would affect not just the humans above ground, but the moles below it. How was the queen mole to continue her work for their community without the trees absorbing psychic energy from other realities? She would no longer be able to sit in the moonlight and channel energy.

'He decided to approach the head gardener. If defenses against flooding were not kept in place, the water meadows and river could break their banks and flood the estate.

'What can I do with the young Master?' he despaired. 'He just won't listen. The lawns must be pristine and the riverbanks straight. Everything so still and perfect, everything in its place.'

'The moles revolted. Every son and daughter, uncle and aunt, nephew and niece dug a hole in the neat lawn leading to the surface. Fine, grained earth potted the neat lawns in mounds.

'The outraged master declared war.

'Three young males were turned into a mole-skin waistcoat. Seven elderly females were crafted into a pair of fine trousers. Others became soft gloves and dusters, employed by the maids in the big house. Finally, a newborn was skinned to adorn the hat of a new under-gardener.

'The king of the moles was distraught. Using his system of tunnels, he eavesdropped on whispers from the vaulted hallways, suggestions among the crystal chandeliers and orders from the huge oak desk in the young masters' study. He detected the low voice of the chief mole-catcher.

'Yet the king mole and the mole-catcher came to an agreement. When the waters rose above the riverbanks in Autumn, the king mole would present himself for capture. Given the choice of drowning him in the swirling waters of the flood-prone Parrett, burning him on a pyre of logs inside Glastonbury Tor or dropping him from the cliffs at Cheddar Gorge, the young master would be persuaded to choose another method of dispatch: to bury him alive.

'And so, when the rains came, the young master's heirlooms, antique carpets and family portraits were washed downstream from the big house. Items of bespoke hand-made furniture bobbed in the current. There were no longer any mole tunnels to channel the water away. No oak roots held back the tide. The young Master could only watch as his inheritance floated away.

'Meanwhile, the mole-catcher counted his coins and the king and queen of the moles relocated to Burrow Mump, a local hill raised well above the waterline. Once there, they raised a family less reliant on the vagaries of a youthful heir.'

I thought about the young Lord and his disregard for the natural course of the river or work of the trees, his search for perfection. In many ways, I too was my own worst enemy. I needed to let my old defences go, so a new self could emerge. One that was not hostile to nature. One that was not hostile to my own nature.

The storyteller read my mind. 'At your birth the stars were in alignment, setting in motion the events which would include the landmarks and crossroads of your life. The hour of that particular day contained the solar information necessary for your symphony to commence.

'Now the conditions are ripe for a transformation to occur. You must ask the right question, listen to the stories, shift your focus and react when the cyclical motion of time says it is right. Healing will involve your family and community. For those with shared thoughts and common beliefs can have an influence over everyone with a common DNA. Leo, where we sit today, the land of your father and of your birth, contains embedded within it the forms that those thoughts take. When the truth is revealed about the hidden patterns working in your subconscious mind or the underworld, you can access the life-force, a secret destiny, your intuition.'

Like the young but arrogant master, I would use any excuse not to show vulnerability. For me, Somerton was a place to learn about ambition and cold reality, concerned with status, security and money.

He continued. 'It was Lancelot's adultery with Guinevere which made him fail the Grail quest. As with the young master, Lancelot did not hallow the four grails – stone, sword, lance and cauldron (or personal destiny, justice, directed will and contentment) – and bought down Arthur's round table. But all was not lost as Merlin prophesied, Sir Galahad, Lancelot's son, was destined to become the best knight in the world, surpass his father in valor and be successful in his search for the Holy Grail!'

Then as we sat on Brockle hill, overlooking the river Cary, the old man took out his drum. He played rhythms to re-enchant the lands around.

'Ceremony reawakens the relationship between Man and the Fae. It allows the ancestors to speak. Now, it is time to honour the lands of your birth. To believe it is worth trying to find the grail again.

'To do this you will need – quite simply – to take energy from below your feet and absorb the skies above. Whenever you feel sapped and depleted, this power source will be all around you.' I had to trust myself to the stars and the land beneath my feet. My limbs felt impossibly light. There was something else, too. A ringing of bells that I wasn't sure anyone but I could hear.

Virgo, August 24th – September 23rd

Virgo represents harvest time both literally and metaphorically – what needs to manifest in life and what steadying influences are necessary.

Virgo is associated with the planet Mercury and the sixth house. Mercury symbolizes flow, new beginnings and change. It passes information through the nervous system and in the outside world by communication. The sixth house reflects the ability of the individual to discriminate – in health and work. It represents employees and health issues.

Associated places: Keinton Mandeville, Stickle Bridge, Wimble Toot, Babcary, Wheathill, Ansford

Chapter Three – Park Pond

It was the Autumn Equinox, the time of the fertility rites of the Mystery Groves. The gentle, undulating landscape around Babcary beckoned. I drove down the Fosse Way to the River Cary via Stickle Bridge – this effigy's broomstick, trident or wheat-sheaf – and onto Ansford near her skirt to visit my mother who lives against the backdrop of Lodge Hill.

The area held a fascinating history. How Druidic sexual practices encouraged the world to regenerate itself. Ancient rites, performed by a Priestess, set free an electrical and a magnetic energy, to allow contact with the spirit worlds. The constellation of the Southern Cross being visible in the northern hemisphere 6,000 years ago – a 'mandorla' or almond shape symbolising the divine feminine.

If Spica, the brightest star of the Virgo constellation translates as 'ear of wheat' – a euphemism for a furrow – then those furrows were made for new seedlings at the rising of the constellation of the Plough. In such a way, fertility was ensured.

As I drew up in Castle Cary, I hailed Phil, the blind man stood by the town's old horse pond. He chatted in his slow Somerset drawl about life before he was overtaken by permanent night. Then he gestured toward the water with his white stick. 'This pond is the source of the Cary. It flows through Cary Moor, across Somerton Moor and down, in an artificial channel called the King's Sedgemoor Drain, to the sea at Bridgwater.'

Somehow, I already knew that water – holy water, along with our blood, spit and sperm – represented the mother of all life, holding memories and the opportunity to develop intuition. Perhaps, as the moon effects the tides, it was water that governed my internal, emotional weather? It was then I noticed the old storyteller was standing behind Phil, beside the bronze, open-winged swan. He wore a cloak replete with black-feathered ruff. The long garment swept around him, a shield against the inclement weather. Tied to his waist was a drawstring bag with symbols apparently burned into its leather sides.

'In Arthurian legend, Virgo is represented by Guinevere, meaning White Eve and Eve the Giver of All. She is the 'ideal woman' to Leo's 'ideal man.' Goddess of nature and Triple Goddess of Earth, Sea and Moon, Guinevere is Mother of all life, who devours her own children and is both old and young, cruel and kind. Guinevere, and thus Virgo, represents both purity and harvest. She is the sign under whose auspices we objectively criticize and analyse the results of our past actions.'

Take the story of King Vortigern and Merlin.

'Following numerous acts of outrage and murder, King Vortigern sat on his assumed throne. With his country under the sway of barbarian tribes, he could only watch as they ravaged his lands and people. Calling on magicians to advise him, he erected an impregnable tower to lift him from the dangers that lay at all sides. Yet build as they might, the earth always swallowed the builders' endeavors. Summoning the same magicians to him, he was instructed to find a youth who had never had a father and then sprinkle his blood at the tower's foundations.

'It happened that two young men were quarrelling at the city gate. 'Damn your eyes,' one of them said, advancing towards the other. 'You dare question my lineage? I am of royal blood on both my father's and mother's sides. You, Merlin, were squired by dogs in the absence of a father.'

'It may be so, Dabutius, that you possess royal blood. But the Gods never endowed you with wisdom or the wit to make you good company.'

'The two looked set to come to blows.

'My friend,' one of the magicians intervened, 'I would be very interested to hear your mother's account of her son's genesis. Perhaps the two of you might settle this matter by addressing her directly.'

'You will find her in St Peter's church,' said Merlin.

'This nun, the daughter of the King of Dimetia, was hauled from her cloisters and presented before King Vortigern.

'By your own life and mine, I don't dissemble for the sake of modesty,' she began. 'I say only this – as I was once with my companions in our chamber, there appeared to me the most beautiful man who embraced me eagerly in his arms and kissed me; after a little time, he vanished from my sight. Following this appearance, he would often talk with me when I sat alone, without any visible appearance. After haunting me a long time in this manner, at last he lay with me in the shape of a man and left me with child.'

'An incubus!' Vortigern declared. 'Inhabiting the area between moon and Earth, possessing elements of angel and elements of men. Whenever it pleases them, they assume human shape and lie with women.'

'Merlin tired of this conversation. 'Pray inform us of the reason for our presence here. Incubus or not, I fear we are in for a lengthy evening.'

When he heard the magicians' claims, Merlin acted decisively.

'Bring all your magicians before me, and I shall demonstrate their falsehoods.'

'To the king, he entreated his workmen dig into the ground at the foot of the tower. 'They will find a pool which causes the foundations to sink. Drain this pool and you will discover two hollow stones, each containing a sleeping dragon.'

'The instructions of the young man were carried out, and those present watched as a white and a red dragon took to the sky only to embrace each other in a death-grip while belching fire.'

Talk of dragons seemed familiar to me. In the dark of night or in a trance state, mythical beasts and cartoon characters – Snow White, Noddy and Pinocchio, dwarves and elves – appeared. There were others – grey monks knelt in long lines with hands tied behind their backs, garish sailors falling from the ship's rigging, rows of ghostly meat hooks in an abattoir, processions of robots, plodding elephants and a devil dressed in vivid red.

I felt like the children of Lir. A curse had been put on me too, and I had to endure it until enough time passed and the stone lock holding me in place crumbled away. Old feelings seemed to be locked deep inside. In my sacrum it was waterlogged and sour. Yet the storyteller seemed excited. 'You will get to experience the story of Merlin. We will work with those things that oppose us and disclose the truth. Working with magic, we will join the two parts of the brain and make darkness and light one.'

At his side lay a harp and a drum.

'On the journey you will meet a wise human who will offer advice and clarity. You will experience a complete realization – a new dawn. We will travel in the sister world of Midgard, the Norse Earth and the waking consciousness where the four treasures of the *Tuatha Dé Danann* still reside, one in each direction representing different skills.'

A hand reached inside the leather bag at his waist. 'The rune Dagaz sits in Muspleheim, a spirit place of fire and light: the world of the Ragnarok, or the end of the world. Go south once you get to the enchanted forest of *Broceliande* which holds the Norse world tree.'

I saw a great forest in which tiny, joyous people populated the trees. Two hooded guardians waved me through a crystal vortex – a portal. A luminous bride was returning from battle on a magnificent, black warhorse as if a queen. The whole army celebrated. I saw that the horse represented the land. The bride was bringing home the divine feminine. Then, as I was dancing on a road to the sun made of a thousand swans' wings, the Norse Goddess of the sun, Sunna came back.'

As his drum beat softened, the storyteller leaned in and whispered.

'The spirits have shown you images – little people, fairies, gnomes and elves, magical animals, pure light, gold and fabulous jewels. You have work to do in our waking world, to help make this your reality. By making use of this new intuition, releasing the things trapped in the past, you can create this new reality for yourself.

'A Saturnine influence is required to confront the Dragons within. These are an embodiment of positive and negative polarity. The pool of ancestral images must be shattered to liberate the internal powers. Only then will you be granted entry to a different time and space - to a flow of images and potent symbols.'

I re-opened my eyes. A bad taste pervaded my mouth. Fleeting images of Angela came – sat in my armchair, clutching a drink. Always defensive, unable to ask, never expecting to receive... it was as if now she began to let go her hold on me. Somehow the trickster spirit had done its work, through me.

The old man nodded sagely. 'When you were sick as a small child, a portion of your psyche started to rule your life. Initially, it protected you; but based on false knowledge and shadowy memories, it soon became corrosive. As with King Vortigern, you need to access this stagnant pond inside yourself, to release the two dragons held there. You have built a fortress on inadequate foundations. A construct founded on fear and force which only a keenly intelligent external agency may destroy. This agency is Merlin.

'At the end of his life, Merlin fell in love with Vivian or Morgan-Le-Fay, a sorceress who coaxed his magic spells out of him, then used them to imprison the old wizard in a tower of white thorns, in which he remains eternally invisible. Only the sound of his voice – whispering with the wind blowing gently through the trees of the vast forest – comes to those knights who wander through the forests of *Broceliande*, in quest of love or the Holy Grail.'

libra dove

Libra, September 24th – October 23rd

Libra is the balance point where things begin to manifest in an external sense. This is where we start to function outside of ourselves or interact with the living environment.

Libra is associated with the planet Venus and the seventh house. Venus is associated with the sensations — touch, sight, hearing, taste and smell — which help us to build a sense of inner security. The seventh house concerns the interaction between two people. It represents competition, known enemies and committed relationships.

Associated places: Barton St David, Baltonsborough Flights, Tootle Bridge

Barton St David Church

Chapter Four – Barton St David Church

Barton St David church was where I was to meet the storyteller. The village, set on the River Brue, is adjacent to Keinton Mandeville, on the witch's petticoats, and situated to the north-east of Somerton's lion. Glastonbury, a town where in ancient times a constant liturgy was recited, a perpetual choir enchanting the surrounding landscape, lay within six miles. As we walked up the path a rainbow arched over the octagonal tower of the village church.

Inside the church's cool walls, a picture of David, Jewish king and bard, playing his harp, greeted us. The storyteller spoke. 'The harp represents the Holy Grail and is the fifth treasure of the *Tuatha Dé Danann*. It carries the notes of all vibration.'

Turning lightly on his feet to face me, the storyteller whispered conspiratorially, 'Light, or the electromagnetic spectrum, travels at a higher, faster vibration than sound. It distorts and transcends our sense of time and with higher frequencies – blue and violet – an electric current is produced. Visualizing and embodying these high octaves can affect material manifestation and be used for healing.'

He continued, 'On the zodiac, the Libran dove is where Arthur is flooded with self-recognition. Three bars of light represent the Lance in the Grail procession and so his inspiration.'

An image of Graham came. At dawn, we had enjoyed a makeshift breakfast of leftovers from the fridge and a flask of hot tea. Soft rain fell in the silence, before children or cricketers could descend. The air felt still and dry beneath the vast oak's canopy, as the warmth of a new day crept in.

We watched as the sun rose from the skyline. As Graham turned towards me, his eyes seemed to alter in colour. They were strangely animated, full of a yearning to connect with what was in front of him. 'How is he doing this? What is he feeling?' I wondered. I had heard of this phenomenon in those able to love someone or something fully.

And so it was I found myself in an in-between world. I was the dove in Arthurian legend, flying through the Grail Castle Hall, a waterspout linking sea and sky. Or was that Graham?

From the church we set out for the zodiac's centre, the abode of the water-serpent Draco. Here he guards the orchard, tail dangling towards the constellation of Virgo. His gullet corresponds with the four stars of Ursa Minor – the hole in which the Earth's axis found its bearings. Draco plays a key part in the marriage of the Sun and the Moon.

Sat beneath one of the four quarter-marker trees, one in each of the four directions – north, south, east and west – the storyteller played sweet harp music. I heard only murmurs, as he listed a long string of stars, planets and constellations – *Draco*, the *Lunar Nodes*, Saturn, the *Beehive Cluster, Ursa Major*, Neptune, Jupiter, Mars, *Lucifer's bright star*, the *Corona Borealis, Buddha's Star*, the *Pleiades, Big Dipper, Antares, Ursa Minor*, the stars of *Hercules, Orion, Sirius and Ophiuchus*. Then, silent, he bore witness to how the Earth wished to react.

'This is a tale of the planets and the Gods.

'The old Irish sea God, affiliated with the *Tuatha Dé Danann*, Manannán mac Lir, will come to your rescue. He is the ruler of the Underworld who ferries souls to the afterlife.

'In time, you will stand where the star Aldebaran sets. It is known as Buddha's Star, the Star of Illumination, God's Eye, the Red Star and the Eye of Revelation – regarded as a fortunate star, it portends riches and honours. It marks our bull's hoof. In stellar myth, this star holds the vision. The Pleiades fall on the bull's collar and provide the blueprint for human consciousness. These stars are responsible for our genetic and spiritual heritage and according to a vision accredited to Merlin, the dissolution of our reality as a great cycle of the solar system closes.

'As night falls on this chapter of your life, you will search for Sirius or the Dog-Star, once used by the Egyptians to mark the start of the New Year.'

Then, naked as the day of his birth, he told me a story.

'The Arthurian legends tell of a young man, brought up innocent though of noble blood, who became the grail king. To achieve this divine status, he had only to ask a very particular question.

'His mother, Herzoloda, had married for love. Gahmuret was a good man and strong. Despite being king, he insisted on earning his way in the world rather than taking it as his due. When Gahmuret was killed in a dispute, a grief-stricken Herzoloda took their child into the forest to raise him ignorant of chivalry and the worldly ways that brought about her husband's death. This royal boy, named Beau Fils, was skilled with the bow yet would weep to see a robin die. He worshipped the Christian God and feared his nemesis.

'One day, mistaking their hoof beats for the devil, Beau Fils stood transfixed as three knights in flashing armour, adorned with feathers and with bells ringing at their knees, appeared. Beau Fils fell to the ground as if before angels. On their instruction, and made up as a fool, Beau Fils took javelin in hand and rode off to the court of King Arthur.

'On the way, he had many adventures in love and chivalry, and learned his real name. 'You are Parzival,' his aunt told him. '*One who pierces the valley*. You are of royal birth and my own husband died defending your lands.

'Aware of his identity, Parzival now took direction from Anfortas, the Fisher King, to reach King Arthur's court. Upon his entrance, Lady Cunneware burst into laughter, fulfilling a prophecy that Parzival would become the best knight in the world. It earned her a flogging. When Parzival avenged her, he took for his own the slain Red Knight's fiery red horse.

'In time, Parzival received instruction on the ways of a knight: to let mercy ride alongside daring and to forbear too many questions. Like his father, he rejected the trappings of knighthood – the hand of his mentor's daughter, a castle, a way of life. He wanted to earn his way. So it was the independent-minded Condwiramurs who became his wife. When she was pregnant with their second son, Parzival set forth on his quest for the castle of the Holy Grail.

'Following directions from a man fishing at the centre of a still lake, Parzival was ready to fulfil his destiny. The castle stood before him. Every eye fell upon him as he entered the huge hall. The Fisher King reclined on his throne in a magnificent sable coat. There in the shadows, Parzival noticed an even older crippled king – one who had received his position by inheritance, not actions. The Fisher King was visibly in pain from a wound in his groin, and Parzival's head spun with questions.

'A procession of maidens bore candles. Tokens were presented to the king – a lance dripping with blood, then a sword forged in heaven. Finally, appeared the Grail itself, borne aloft on a cloth of gold by the radiant Queen Repanse de Schoye. Parzival knew that if he asked the right question, the ailing king would be set free. But he failed to speak.

'After some time, the king politely announced it was time to retire.

'Parzival's dreams were tortured. His sense of duty and fear of social opinion had turned him from his course. In the morning, the castle rooms were empty and silent. He departed without ceremony. Parzival had lacked the heart to ask the question that would heal the king and redeem the waste land.

'When he returned to Arthur's court, the sorceress Cundrie berated the King for welcoming one who had brought shame upon   . the Round Table. On hearing her words, Parzival resolved to locate the castle of the Holy Grail once more. Riding forth, he renounced his mother's God to spend five years in the desert of his soul. He encountered Hatred, Rejection and Ego, Pride, Suffering, Pain and Deprivation. Hostility met his every turn. At one point, a Temple Knight riding a horse branded with turtle doves told him to leave or face death. A procession of pilgrims accosted him: 'How dare you ride in knightly armour on Good Friday?'

'Eventually, he fell upon a holy man to whom the spirits spoke directly. 'Some years ago, a fool came to the Grail castle and made a terrible mistake,' this man said. 'Now, he is cursed by God.' The weight of the statement broke Parzival.

'Yet it was under this man's guidance that he began to comprehend the spiritual life. Following this learning, Parzival happened upon a man on horseback. Only when the two were engaged in battle did he realise he was combatting his own half-brother, Feirefiz – a half black and half white man. Together, the two rode with the Sorceress Cundrie to the Grail castle and now Parzival voiced the correct question: 'What is wrong?'

'The Fisher King was immediately healed and Parzival became the new Grail King.'

'The Parzival story tells us that even though we are often told otherwise, a second chance to heal, to regain our intuition – our holy grail – can appear. This will require sacred music, song, chant and melody, along with colour, red, orange, yellow, green, blue, indigo and violet. With access to higher vibrations, other levels of consciousness will come - the worlds of the Fae and *Tír fo Thuinn*.

'Like the medieval monks, you will need to literally enchant the land around you.'

scorpio

Scorpio, October 24th – November 22nd

Scorpio represents the potential power of destruction and the propensity for both good and evil. It is traditionally symbolized by the lizard, which is the lowest creature on the evolutionary scale and the eagle, one who realizes the full potential of Scorpio. The modern symbol is the scorpion.

Scorpio is associated with the planets Mars and Pluto and the eighth house. Mars is the planet of constructive and destructive energies and the way in which we project ourselves. Pluto is the planet of transformation and regeneration. In the process of breaking down the cells of the body or vegetation, new energy is released. The eighth house concerns materials gained through others and deep emotional giving, along with death, sex, taboo, ancestors, magic and the occult.

Associated places: Parbrook, Hell Ditch, Lottisham, Stone, Alford, Hornblotten

Hornblotton Tower

Chapter Five – Hornblotton Church

It was a dark November afternoon when we entered the grounds of St Peter's church at Hornblotton. The gale-force winds and heavy rain were signs of an intense depression above us.

Outside the gate, as the heavens opened, the storyteller pinched the top of a nettle and held it in his hand. Then, as we took the steps onto hallowed ground, he spat, sharing his DNA. 'This earth has long been sacred to our ancestors, whether Christian vicars, Druidic priests or hunter-gatherers. These nettles that so often appear in bombsites and battle grounds are good for all manner of healing.'

Rain streamed down his face as he continued. 'Here, in Scorpio, we stagger under the burdens of our past and have to let go. This is where we die, so a sovereign-self – able to rule with fullness of body, heart and spirit – may emerge.

'Death, whether a bereavement or a shamanic death of part of the personality, is an important part of the journey. Some believe the death of the body occurs in the middle and not at the end of a cycle. It is merely a portal to another life; part of an evolutionary process, much like the initiate's spiral or knight's quest.'

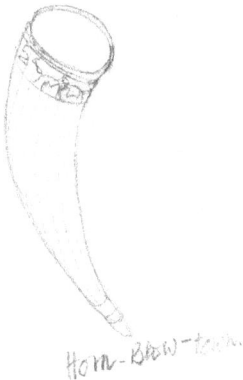

Horn-Blow-town

Beneath an ancient yew, he spoke again. I would have turned, except that most often he spoke to the air before him without meeting my eyes. In his hand was a bedraggled drawing. 'Hornblotton used to boast a horn, it's said. A blast from the church tower warned the people of rising waters. *Horn-blow-town*.'

In my mind, I lifted a clapper on the old, displaced bell. The Hornblotton church had clearly been rebuilt in a slightly different location. Only a stump of the old, medieval tower remained in the churchyard. Here on the original church site, standing stones had been set to call up water, often being built into the church walls themselves. The water was drawn towards the weight of the building.

'A church tower is something that amplifies the energy of the land – be it feminine or masculine, water or rock, crystal or earth – within the boundaries of its parish. Agriculturally speaking, employing geomancy – the use of power places – can lead to significant increases in production. Should the land need sun or water energy, an appropriate structure can be helpful.

'Bending the physical realm, some believe it is possible to stand on the power point of a tower and connect from one church to another – a kind of system of beacons by which one may discuss pressing concerns.'

The weather front passed overhead, exposing a red-tiled roof and squat, square tower both gleaming with moisture in the weak rays of late afternoon sunlight. Beyond the orange oolite stone portal, decorated sgraffito walls and an early electric clock awaited us. Given permission, we passed up the aisle towards the choir and altar. Dusk was dulling the stained-glass windows and the dimly-lit figures carved on the pew stanchions. 'In time, we will see the figure of Lucifer, the light-bringer who once made Scorpio's constellation resplendent.'

I looked past the open door for a sign of the evening star.

His voice interrupted my reverie. 'Saint Peter is the Patron Saint of Popes and Rome, along with net-makers, ship-builders and fishermen, cobblers and people with foot problems. When Jesus was on trial before the Sanhedrin, Peter denied knowing him three times. Yet he became regarded as the first leader of the Roman church, a man entrusted with the 'keys to heaven and hell'. Following his martyrdom, the scribes altered the stories to suit the prevailing political climate.

'Maybe the story of St Peter and the Scorpio landscape – one of destruction and remodeling – is not so different from your own. Your internal scribes have given you an altered story with which to work. To achieve any form of rebirth requires a death first.'

Childhood illness did still stay harbored within me. Long days sitting in playgroup, safely confined in my mother's inventive contraption; or being carried about. I still stored these experiences inside me but had not yet died to that world.

When I was still a baby, paralysis, isolation and pain became real. From the outside, I was pitiable: high fevers, a salmon-pink rash and swollen neck joints that became unworkable. All too often, I was fetched for a hateful trip down the long white corridors to be injected with a painful, greasy needle. A part of me wanted to die.

Afterwards, I came home and tried to walk. It was too soon and my condition flared up. The Doctor lambasted my mother. Since then, I had lost the ability to experience the felt sense. I was numb to the world around me. Part of my psyche was undeveloped, still trapped in those barely understood days.

The storyteller lay star-shaped on the floor. After a while, he sat up and took out his drum. The rudimentary beat seemed to respond to his words, to what he had heard and felt.

'We may need to visit the realm of *Hel*, at the base of the world tree, to disperse these unwanted energies,' he said to the background tapping, 'However, the bridge that crosses the river *Gjoll* is guarded by a giant Maiden.'

I felt ready to surrender myself and experience a first death. The storyteller read my mind.

'King Arthur, Sir Accolan of Gaul, and King Uriens, the husband of the enchantress Morgan le Fay, followed the track of a great hart into the depths of a vast forest. So great was the chase the horses felt dead beneath the huntsmen. Night was falling and, in need of shelter, they walked in the tracks of the hart. It lay dying on the bank of a river, a hound at its throat and others swiftly coming in full bay. The chase complete, Arthur killed the hart.

'To his surprise, a small vessel appeared, bedecked with flowing sails of silk. It touched land on the sandy bank. Not a living person was to be seen on board. 'What a marvelous ship. Let us enter,' Arthur commanded. The darkness lifted as torches flared brightly from the ship's side.

'From its depths, twelve beautiful damsels emerged and fell to their knees before King Arthur. 'Follow us, noble sir.' Inside were silken hangings and a table overflowing with fine food and the rarest wine. Replete and escorted to their chambers, the hunters fell into a deep and dreamless sleep.

'King Uriens awoke to find himself in bed with his wife, Morgan Le Fay. Arthur's plight was less comfortable. He awoke in utter darkness – in a dungeon filled with groaning knights – and knew a foul enchantment was upon him. 'We are all the victims of an evil-hearted villain,' he ventured.

'His supposition was correct. Sir Ontzlake, a worthy knight, awaited satisfaction over a feud with his brother the coward and traitor Sir Damas. Sir Ontzlake would fight any knight prepared to take up the quarrel since his own brother was too faint-hearted to bear arms. The knights in the dungeon told Arthur that they had chosen imprisonment rather than represent such a scoundrel in so base a quarrel.

'I will fight rather than perish in this prison!' shouted Arthur, into the darkness confining him.

'With that, a fair damsel appeared bearing a light. 'If you fight, you will be delivered. Those are my master's terms.' And so the shapeshifter known as Morgan Le Fay departed. An agreement struck, Arthur prepared to do battle and to free the imprisoned knights.

'Meanwhile Accolan, one of Morgan Le Fay's lovers, awoke to find himself in great peril on the precipice of a deep well-side. He crossed himself and swore to destroy all enchantresses, if he were to survive. Beside him a large dwarf saluted him. 'Tomorrow it will be your task to fight a knight of the greatest prowess. Morgan Le Fay has sent you Arthur's sword, Excalibur, with its magical scabbard, so you may win.'

'I shall do her bidding. These crafts and enchantments, are they are of her doing?'

'She has prepared them to bring on this battle.'

'And so, it was that Arthur and Accolan were set to meet on the battlefield. As they rode forward a fair damsel came to Arthur, bringing him a sword like Excalibur, with a scabbard that seemed the very same. 'Morgan le Fay sends you your sword, for the great love she bears you,' said the messenger, 'and hopes it may do you worthy service in the fray.'

'Arthur took it and thanked her, never dreaming that he had been treated falsely. But the sword that was sent him was just a brittle and worthless blade. The scabbard a base counterfeit of that magic one, which he who wore, could lose no blood. Both these precious items, in brotherly trust, had he given to the care of his faithless sister.

The storyteller stood upright. 'King Arthur survived the battle and recovered Excalibur but the sword's scabbard, a magical key, was forever lost and with it his protection. The sword is used to separate, disentangle, dismember or cut constrictions – in so doing, it releases our creative, protective or destructive forces. Excalibur rules the warrior self and rulership and Arthur's scabbard protected this fiery passion.

'For you, little fires – hurts, betrayals, misuses of power – have become the stars in your inner world; a night sky only the dwarves, representing the senses, can read. Trickery and enchantment have altered the deep structure of your brain, redirected your neural pathways, which now stand sentry, like a gatekeeper. To make up for your loss, different areas of your brain, of your psyche, took over.'

I was imprisoned, had lost my way and along with it, part of me had died. Past experiences had left me entrapped.

Arthur too, was gravely wounded by his son Mordred, whose name means 'moderate, within bounds.' Arthur is Sagittarius, and Mordred Scorpio. In the legends, Arthur was ferried past the Isle of Avalon down the Brue and through the eastern portal at East Pennard, where he *died to the world*.' In this end was his beginning. I would be walking that way soon.

Sagittarius

Sagittarius, November 23rd – December 21st

In Sagittarius we remember our heritage and its prevailing social and cultural patterns. This sign, represented by the horse or the Archer, a symbol of intuition, helps us to develop a true aim towards our goal.

Sagittarius is associated with the planet Jupiter and the ninth house. Jupiter concerns the processes of expansion, optimism and goodwill. Together with Saturn it represents the end results of our experiences through the nervous system, the senses and the muscular system. The ninth house is associated with the public expression of our personal thoughts and organizing them into a philosophy or religion we can live our lives by. It is a spiritual house connected with advanced learning and long journeys.

Associated places: West Pennard, Breech Lane, West Bradley, Arthur's Bridge

Sagitarius

Chapter Six – Arthur's castle

Back at my cottage, Angela's expression was friendly but intense.
'Builders' or something more exotic?' I asked as she followed me
to the kitchen. As the kettle boiled, I felt her eyes tracking my
movements: taking the tea from its caddy; rooting for the delicate
bone-china cup and saucer covered with poppies and forget-me-knots
she liked so much; pouring the brew. The hairs on my neck tingled.

Through the window, the trees tossed. Mimi sat on the sill patiently
awaiting a flicker of movement; insect, fledgling, field mouse.
In a curious way, the old cottage resembled me. Set solidly in its
landscape, it seemed always to have been there. The well-worn
floorboards and stone walls held the resonance of previous occupants.
Sometimes the strange warmth made my thighs buzz and my hips want
to dance.

So why was I itching to get away?

The next day found me near West Pennard. Yet another turning
point. The landscape of quaint country cottages and family hearths,
the ploughed farmland ready for Spring drilling and the bustling
pubs told me so. It was all too neat and homely. Something in me had
to die.

A seasonal earthy smell of damp soil wafted through the air. These
waterlogged lands had once been flooded. Here on South Moor,
before medieval monks drained and redirected the course of the river
Brue around the Isle of Avalon, the *Cetus* Whale of Arthurian legend
swallowed Arthur, only to disgorge him after three days.

The storyteller was dressed as a country man, complete with family
kilt. He was a picture in his moleskin waistcoat and Wellington boots.

'King Arthur, associated with Sagittarius, is the wintering sun in decline. As seasons change, he is dragged into the underworld to face past demons. This hero with a thousand faces frees us from our chains. His sacrifice leads to rebirth in the depths of our subconscious.'

Death and rebirth. Not a new thought.

'A voluntary sacrifice is required. To lay to rest the seemingly impossible trials of childhood along with their echoes. To allow your less-conscious parts to grow in awareness.'

'Well,' I thought to myself. 'This is it.'

Then he declared, 'King Pelias desired dominion over all Thessaly.

'It was nothing to him to imprison his half-brother Aeson, the King of Iolcos, and kill his attendants. When Aeson's wife gave birth, she knew she had to fall on her wits or her new son, Jason, would be murdered to prevent his revenge. She and her handmaids dropped to their knees, as if the child were stillborn. With Pelias convinced, she smuggled the babe to the cave of the centaur, Chiron who raised him in ignorance of his birthright.

'But the king had nagging doubts. An oracle told him to beware a stranger wearing one sandal, and it had the ring of truth about it.

'Meanwhile, Jason learned his status. As he approached Iolcos, he lost his sandal assisting the disguised Goddess Hera across the river, receiving her blessing. Pelias beheld this stranger who would rid him of his kingdom, and thought fast. All smiles, he dispatched him on a suicide mission before he might return to claim his kingdom. The quest? To retrieve the Golden Fleece.

'In Classical myth, as Phrixus and his sister Helle were fleeing their murderous stepmother, they mounted a ram given to them by Zeus, king of the gods, and took to the sky. Endowed with reason and speech, it moved through the air effortlessly. Yet Helle slipped from its back and was drowned in the stretch of water known ever since as the Hellespont. On reaching Colchis, at the Eastern end of the Black Sea, Phrixus sacrificed the golden ram to Zeus and gave its fleece to King Aeetes in gratitude for his safe passage. The delighted king hung it from a tree, where it was guarded by a dragon which never slept.

'Jason had the right equipment and the right men. His fifty-oared ship was built by Argo, a talented carpenter, and its benches carried a cast of heroes including Castor and Polydeuces, Heracles and Orpheus, not to mention Theseus, King of Athens. In her prow, the Argo held a piece of timber from the Dodona forest which was endowed with speech and aligned with the stars to aid navigation.

'What Jason had not anticipated was that his crew might demonstrate every aspect of human strength and weakness and need to depend upon inner guidance when pitted against monsters, men and the unfavourable elements. They fell for the women of Lemnos who, having deserted Aphrodite, lived an existence entirely without men. Their ship was attacked by an earth-born monster with six arms. The crewman Hylas was bewitched by a water nymph. In Bythinia, Polydeuces killed king Amycus in a boxing match, arousing the anger of his tribe. The crew freed a blind seer tormented by Harpies for divulging too many secrets and sent a white dove across the Symplegades to calm the waters between its two gigantic clashing rocks. When their navigator Tiphys fell asleep, they were attacked by the Stymphalian Birds whose lethal feathers were tipped with bronze.

'Finally arriving in Colchis, the Goddess Hera saw to it that Jason fell in love with the sorceress Medea, daughter of King Aeetes. Medea helped Jason vanquish the dragon which guarded the precious trophy and as they made off with the fleece on the Argo, she cut up her brother and scattered the pieces of his body into the water. King Aeetes, stricken with grief, called his fleet to a stop and gathered up the dismembered pieces.

'The return journey proved perilous. Sirens called to them from treacherous rocks. Thetis, the sea nymph, carried them safely past a six-headed monster and a deadly whirlpool. Hera's blessing had seen Jason through. He married Medea on the island of Drepane before returning to Iolcos to claim the throne.'

With that, the old man held out his arms as if they were wings. He drew on his medicine cloak, covered in the black plumage of a chough. Then a red-beaked, feathery bird mask and blood-red shoes appeared. His nose became extended, almost beak-like, whilst his eyes were piercing blue beads filled with an intense light.

'This king will not die, but by magic art will turn into a raven and ascend to another level.

'We will find a vehicle for divine intervention. Seek the help of the gods, the goddesses, the ancestors and the animals to transform and evolve. Let the overused parts of your ego fade into the background.' The rhythmic sound of a drum and his gentle voice lulled me into another world.

'Past lives are holding you entrapped in this one. This is the same for us all. Unresolved experiences are the reason we return again and again to a physical form from the land of the dead. Now, we will journey to the realm of the ancestors, into *Hel* itself and look them in the face.'

First, I saw the image of a lowly peasant at Bannock Burn with his stomach blown apart. A once pretty wife and bonny children wept amongst the purple heathers, now hungry and homeless as disembodied memories – of highland dancing, music and merriment – floated past, no longer connected to their lives. The bloody battle, a Scottish victory for Robert the Bruce against the army of King Edward II of England, had left a mournful scene: independence for Scotland but grief and loss for the nation's families. Then a coquettish prostitute inveigled men to her bed as a young man dangled by one ankle on a long rope. Elders stood patiently on a wooden platform high above him. I saw a corpulent king dressed in ermine, fed on privilege and others' labour. A 17th century sea captain in gold braid and tricorn hat, carrying a musket, led his fleet into foreign lands to decimate the population and destroy the earth that fed them. Finally, a sea-stained watchman kept lookout with his spyglass, clasping the rigging of a whaling ship.

By this time, I no longer needed the storyteller to tell me my pretty cottage, with its chipped saucers and antique throws, was my castle; that it housed my past, both the good and not so good; or that a hero must accept her failings and seek help from otherworldly entities familiar with the soul lessons we need to learn.

How was a different matter!

Our ancestors developed their psychic abilities for practical needs – finding water and medicinal herbs – by using intermediaries such as encounters with animals and signs from nature. Yet, these ancestors, the keepers of our genetic and cultural memory, also transmit memories of violence, persecution and oppression – trauma. Somehow, I needed to acknowledge this – to speak with them.

'When you gain success, remember not to be over-protective of what seems valuable. Seek the source of creative imagination. When you harmonize your animal- and god-self you will gain access to hidden realities.

'Arthur had to rely on his younger knights to do battle for him. To aim straight like the Archer himself. To be a bear protecting her cub. To sleep until awakened by his country's need.

'It's more than possible to take wrong paths in this life. The human condition is to re-enact or creatively copy what has gone before, whether an ancestral wound passed down the line or a trauma experienced in this lifetime. Constantly seeking a solution, we draw towards us a cast of people to make resolution possible – drawing similar circumstances towards us. Jason's adventures reflect our human dilemma. He quests, like Arthur, for solutions from the inner levels, feeling and intuition, rather than relying on his faculties of will and rational thought.'

capricorn

Capricorn, December 22nd – January 20th

Capricorn embodies the change which comes with time. It represents the extremes of height and depth. Experience is of the essence.

Capricorn is associated with the planet Saturn and the tenth house. Saturn looks inward for experience and learning and searches for the meaning of life through organized processes. The tenth house reflects the outward expression and direction the person takes in life — profession, status, attitude towards authority. Along with the parent of the same sex, crops and the weather.

Associated places: Ponter's Ball, Barrow, Launcherlay Hill, Hearty Moor

Ponter's Ball.

Chapter Seven – Ponter's Ball

I didn't really want to meet the storyteller that cold winter's day. Graham was nowhere to be found and, hermit-like in the Winter Solstice spirit, I had retired under my bed covers. For once Angela came with me. We were heading for the stars of Capricorn, the Great Bear popularly known as the Big Dipper or the Plough – one of the most-recognized constellations in the northern hemisphere.

Up on an ancient earthwork, we stood rigid against the winter winds, the ground sodden beneath our feet and the views shrouded in mist. Visitors from foreign lands would once have gathered here. Known as the horn of Capricorn, or locally as Ponter's Ball, it was another long-disused gateway to Avalon and one which, when referred to as the Golden Coffin, acts as Arthur's grave. Therefore, it marks the time when free-thinking and access to nature and the stars went underground. The old druidic magical culture known as the mysteries of the Unicorn were tortured, burned and decimated by the incoming Romans. The lion on the zodiac represents the new heart of materialism.

Inane chatter like the twittering of love birds entered my awareness. Two young tourists had clambered up the grassy mound and were now listening in. They faced the glass mountain, which hosted one's own reflection, apparently without seeing.

A watch-face glittered on the storyteller's wrist. The turn-ups of his second-hand business suit were damp underneath his tattered gaberdine mac. A deep mossy stain at knee-level showed where he had tripped. A rivulet of water ran down his back from collar to hem.

Ignoring the visitors, he talked sternly. 'The astrological sign of Capricorn is associated with Saturn or Father Time. His gateway comes in cycles of seven years and takes twenty-eight years to complete.

'Saturn affects our experiences on an individual level and governs the ways and values of society. Yet we must experience our life lessons directly, be they grief, victory or true love. Physical engagement is the name of the game.'

I recalled how Saturn teaches us to work hard, to respect our elders and overcome any restrictions placed on us in childhood. It highlights our destiny and brings conflict into our lives when we refuse to learn. It requires us to plumb the extremes of height, depth, passion and self-loathing to achieve rebirth and the changes that come with time.

'We would be wise to take note of Saturn's position in our birth chart and track its course in our lives. Some things are fated.'

The storyteller turned to Angela and held her gaze. After a few minutes he said, 'You must master the challenge of sweetness, learn to take joy from life.'

Then to me, 'The wheel of the zodiac has turned back to the time of your childhood illness. Saturn controls restrictions, responsibility and Karma. Every action you take has a consequence. Saturn represents the inevitable cycle of trial and error.'

His message to the visitors came in another story. One concerning the second-largest planet in the Solar System whose rings reflected the idea of human limitations.

'A miller's daughter stood sweeping the woodchips from her father's backyard. She swayed with the rhythm of her work. Completing her task, she gazed at the mill, once dilapidated and uncared for, but now in good repair.

'Three years before, the miller had been interrupted from his chores by the voice of a devilish man. 'Why trouble yourself to chop wood? I'll make you rich, should you promise me what stands behind your mill.' The miller had come on hard times. So he agreed.

'In three years, I will come and fetch what is mine,' the man said, and the miller went back to his tasks.

'How should it be that the miller recognised that voice all those years later? Was it the curl of his laugh that brought such unease? Or its unannounced quality? Whatever, the three years had now passed and he had come to collect his due – the miller's daughter.

'Though his advances would prove as insubstantial as his laughter.

'Washing herself quite clean, the miller's daughter drew a circle around herself with chalk. Despite his advances, the seething man could not approach her and cried out, 'Take away all water from her so she cannot wash herself, for otherwise I have no power over her.'

'Fearing the worst, her father followed his orders.

'The following morning, as the man advanced, the miller's daughter wept onto her hands till they were quite clean. This time, the man's reaction was more extreme. 'Chop off both her hands, or else I cannot obtain her.'

'The penitent father approached his trembling daughter. 'My child, I am truly sorry,' he said. 'Forgive the wickedness I am about to do you.' Then, binding his daughter's hands behind her back, he severed her hands from her wrists with a swing of the axe.

'For a third time, the man approached. The miller's daughter let fall so many tears, however, that her arms were once again splashed clean. The man was obliged to give her up, but she could no longer remain at her father's mill. Arms bound behind her back, she departed. 'Kind people will give me all that I need,' she said.

'The following night fell, and the daughter came to a royal garden surrounded by lakes. Tormented by hunger, she knelt and prayed. Putting her lips to the water, she was beginning to slake her thirst when an angel descended and gave her passage to the far bank. There, a grove of pear trees stood lit by the moon. Mysteriously, each time the maiden lifted her mouth, a branch would lower itself allowing her to nibble the fruit. A sense of peace came upon her.

'The following morning, when the King came to assess his property, he discovered one of his pears was missing. 'Gardener!' he called. 'Who trespasses here to eat my silver pears?' The gardener shuffled on the spot. 'Last night a spirit with no hands crossed the water and ate one of your pears.'

'That evening, as darkness fell, the King sat with a priest under a tree in the grove. At the chime of midnight, with a stirring of leaves a young woman took her place beside them. 'I am no spirit,' she said, 'but a poor maiden, deserted by all save God alone.' His heart breaking with pity, the King immediately brought her to the palace and ordered silver hands to be constructed for her. For every queen must be in possession of hands.

'After a year passed, the country went to war. The king instructed his mother to write to him should the queen bring forth a child.

'Soon afterwards, the king's mother wrote a letter to her son. *Rejoice, for the queen has given birth to a fine boy!* However, the letter was exchanged for another by hands which had been kept from the miller's daughter despite a bargain being struck. *Despair, for the queen has brought a changeling into the world!* The battle-weary king was distraught when he read the note. Neither did the devil's reply allow room for misunderstanding: *The queen and her child must be killed.*

'As her son had once done, the King's mother now took pity. 'Go forth into the wide world never to return,' she said, binding the new-born upon the queen's back. The young mother wept bitterly as she left the palace. Yet all was not lost. In the midst of the wild forest, she fell to her knees and prayed. Once again, an angel appeared to her, silently leading her to a little cottage over which hung a wooden sign inscribed with the words *Here may everyone live freely.* A snow-white maiden welcomed the queen, and she went inside with her baby. Seven years would pass in this place of safety. During this period, on account of her piety, her hands grew again as before.

'When the king returned from war, he made straight for the bed-chamber where he had long anticipated the sound of his wife's laughter and the first sight of his son. But the bedchamber was bare. Neither could his wife be found in the kitchens or with the maids. When his mother showed him the forged letters, he wept bitterly.

'My beautiful wife is dead!' he wailed. But when his mother revealed the pity she had shown to the queen, the king rejoiced. 'Heaven knows I will find her again!'

'For seven long years, he combed the forest. One morning, thick of beard but steadfast in mind, the king approached a cottage that all but blended into the background. The snow-white maiden came to the door.

'My wife has silver hands,' he told her. 'I have been searching for her without success for this past seven years. She has a son I have never seen.' As he was led into the house, he saw a woman crumbling soil into a flowerpot. Her pink fingers were nimble and pale. 'Merciful God has allowed my hands to grow back,' she told him. A heavy stone lifted from his heart. The king and queens' reunion was a happy one, and their return to the castle with their son was an occasion of great joy. They celebrated their marriage and lived happily till the end of their lives.'

I looked round to Angela, and her eyes met mine. She had clearly heard the same story.

'What did the storyteller mean when he said those things to you?' I asked.

'Oh, I don't know. That I needed to grow back my hands if I was to live happily ever after. Something like that.'

I smiled. Only when the handless woman experienced her life lessons and found wholeness could her transformation occur. Afterwards, she re-found a world in which anything could happen. One that would let her caress and feel again, to *care for* and value life.

At the finish, the storyteller had disappeared as if he had never existed. In my mind I heard the words – not necessarily in his voice – 'During Saturnalia, reality turns on its head for twelve days. Masters become servants, servants masters. Soon, you will need to turn back the clock to draw on energy and symbols related to the golden age of harmony – a time of feasting, sleeping and storytelling.'

Aquarius, January 21st – February 19th

Aquarian symbolism is of Absolute Truth. This sign shows us where we might act with the most originality and show true wisdom.

Aquarius is associated with the planets Uranus and Saturn and the eleventh house. Uranus breaks down the traditional values of the Capricorn ethic. It allows the process of 'individuating'. Saturn looks inward for experience and learning and searches for the meaning of life through organized processes. The eleventh house reflects our creative expression in association with others. It is the house of hopes and wishes.

Associated places: Glastonbury Tor, Chalice Well, Ashwell Lane, Edmund Hill, Paradise Lane

Glastonbury Tor

Chapter Eight – Glastonbury Tor

Sometime that gloomy night, a gray shadow figure came into my dreams. As he walked away, my heart felt as if it might burst. My world flipped upside down. For weeks, Abba's 'The Name of the Game' resounded in my head. Graham's otherworldly guidance urged me to listen, really listen.

Life back in my cottage was chaotic. Sadness permeated and my personality changed. It was as if I lived in a nether world. A profound emptiness enveloped me. Time passed by, with a part of me disconnected from mundane affairs. I did not have the concentration required to engage with life as I had known it before. Weeks existing on hawthorn berry tea.

In the days before Graham's funeral, the storyteller and I visited my ancestor's graves. We set down red roses and sprinkled a nip of whiskey, then drove around my dad's farm reminiscing. By a woodland gate, a red rose glinted from the hedgerow as it looked towards the valley. A hawk circled low over-head.

'The hawk carries a message for you. You shared a deep connection with Graham. He became part of you and you part of him. Your heart perceives the pain of his loss. Yet this will produce a healing chemistry for the body which will radiate out through the *fields* – our auras – and be transmitted to others, be they people, animals or plants; both in this and parallel worlds.

'Grief is necessary for us to accept that something we loved has become a spirit. Without this emotion, a departed loved one or part of your soul cannot arrive where death wants it to go and may become angry with the living. Then it may intrude and become a real nuisance.

'The emotion will help you to feel and re-kindle. Eventually it will even calm you. Let it come. Do what you can to tell Graham's story and complete his affairs in a kindly fashion. This will help. Then let him go. He will have things to do and a transition of his own to manage.'

'Why didn't he tell me?'

'He was a good man, and was only trying to protect you. His death was fated. Have trust in him now.'

I didn't see or hear from the storyteller again for a week or two. I read slowly, learned new information and time passed.

I turned my thoughts to the Phoenix – marker of the end of the world as we know it and representative of new beginnings. We were leaving the Piscean age to enter one ruled by Uranus, the lightning-striker. Uranus's insight into the laws of nature would encourage the highest possible expression of individuality and reject subservience to enforced rules and regulations; it would implement humanitarian values for the benefit of the group as a whole.

One gloomy day, I headed to Glastonbury Tor, the Phoenix's head. Fire energy travels through this place. The Tor rises out of the vast sea moors, with the remains of an old labyrinth path still visible in its steep green slopes. Considered as Avalon, it is the biggest isle in these parts, dwarfing Nyland, Marchey, Panborough, Godney, Meare and Beckery.

'In time – like the phoenix – comes resurrection.' I thought of Graham and my brother and wished they could be here with me now.

Sitting on a wooden bench mid-climb, the storyteller took out a pencil. Below us the hills traced the contours of the Phoenix's body and wings. Chalice Well, with its Blood and white springs, lay at the end of its beak.

'The Tor is like our brain – a spiral castle with labyrinth-like pathways.'

The storyteller shifted position and gestured towards the ruined church tower of the Tor. 'In as much as a church resembles a family, designed to pass on wealth, spiritual knowledge and inherited legacies, it often had a labyrinth at its threshold. Many have now been removed. This was in recognition of the transformative effect that walking of a labyrinth had on a person's psyche, bringing together analytical and intuitive levels of consciousness.'

'The *Prose Edda* tells us of *Ragnarök* – a time of earthquake, famine and great flood decreed by the *Norns*, the female beings who spin the fate of humans.

'Then the Earth will shudder and a rust-red cock raise the dead. A bound giant will break its fetters. A ship named *Naglfar*, built from the nails of corpses, will break onto the high seas. Fenir, the monstrous wolf, will run free, his lower jaw scraping the ground and his upper jaw reaching the sky, flames dancing in his eyes and leaping from his nostrils. In this twilit time, nation will rise against nation, kingdom against kingdom. A great winter will descend. Stars will fall from the sky and the Heavenly powers shake. Yet still the eagle will fly.

'So it is when the labyrinth of our psyche unravels.

'Awoken by the watchman Heimdall's great horn, the Gods will assemble in council. All will quake as giants cross the rainbow bridge, *Bifrost*, to storm *Asgard* and gain entry through its great wall. Parts of the celestial city will become a furnace and *Midgard*, *Jotenheim* and *Nifelheim* burn along with it. Heimdall, the watchman of the gods, will be slain, along with the thunder god Thor and Loki the trickster spirit. Old gods will die alongside giants, monsters and creatures of the underworld.

'Odin, mounted on his eight-legged horse Sleipnir, will consult the well of *Mimir*. *Yggdrasill*, the great Ash, will tremble. Yet two humans hidden in its mighty branches will survive. Following this, there will be a reckoning amongst the gods.

'Then the monstrous wolf Fenir will take Odin's life, only to be revenged by his son Vidar. Using a magical shoe, he will press one foot onto the wolf's bottom jaw and, taking hold of the upper jaw, tear it apart, putting an end to his devastation.

'Vidar will survive along with the sons of Thor who shall inherit their father's hammer. Balder, the God of light, joy and the summer sun, will return from the land of the dead. Then the wand of Honir will foretell what is to come: rulers will live in the heavens at peace, whilst *Nastrond* will house the oath-breakers, murderers and philanderers along with the dragon *Nidhogg* who shall suck the blood from the bodies of the dead.

'And so the cycle will be complete – the same elements of fire and flood that created life will end it. A new world will emerge, a time beyond time, purged of all evil.'

We continued to climb. High up, where an ancient Beacon tree once spread its massive branches, we overlooked the water-logged sea moors. 'This 872-year old male oak was felled on the orders of the church nearly a thousand years ago. It stood where seven energy lines crossed. The male – or Michael – ley line largely follows a buried line of white quartz, whilst the female – Mary – line weaves in and out, following springs, rivers, streams and wells of water.'

The storyteller whispered as if he was far away. 'As with any death it is important to bypass our fear-based limbic brain, forgive ourselves and find compassion, completion and acceptance so our spirits can fly. Ritual helps override the neo-cortex, with which we attempt to understand things, so the reptilian brain can take us through the process.'

He cast a mysterious circle and invoked the spirits. Before us on the ground was a large square of paper; beside it lentils, rice, beans and hundreds and thousands. Perhaps twenty small packets of household goods. Alongside them was a bottle of good red wine and a bottle of white. Flowers of all colours and sizes were in bunches ready for our ceremony. 'These represent health, wealth and happiness. They set our intention to heal the family lines.'

Over the next two hours, each item was carefully added to our mandala until the large square of paper was a burst of colour and heaped like a small hill. At each juncture a toast was raised in celebration. Finally, flower-heads were gently added and a blessing made. Wrapped in beautiful cloth, the ceremonial bundle was ready for its final destination.

The old storyteller took out his runes. He cast them four times. 'The ancestors say this bundle must go into the water. Water represents absolute truth. Like a mother, the ocean will cleanse and heal. On the Full Moon, you must release it to the sea to signify the end and a new beginning of Graham's spiral process. Things left undone will now be completed.

'Our ancestors, the elder race whose role it is to guide the spiritual evolution of the human race, have spoken. It is they, the Fae, who called for this initiatory experience in the Giant realm.

'In time, your emotional life will be reconciled. The Well of Mimir, where Odin sacrificed an eye in exchange for a drink, has taken its price for the wisdom and knowledge gained.'

Pisces, February 20th – March 20th

The Piscean fish represents swimming in a nether world – neither the world we know nor quite another world. It is the struggle of the soul within the body.

Pisces is associated with the planet Neptune and the twelfth house. Neptune – the 'sea of the unconscious' or 'collective unconscious' – seeks to dissolve all boundaries and store experience in symbols. The twelfth house represents our mental and emotional attitudes towards our health, along with the darker side of life, witchcraft and animals big enough to ride.

Associated places: Wearyall Hill, Fishers Hill, Pomparles Bridge, Hulk Moor, Wallyer's Bridge

Holy Thorn
Wearyall Hill

Chapter Nine – Wearyall Hill

A month or so later, I saw the storyteller again.

I was on Wearyall Hill, and half of me didn't want to leave where I was at all. At least I knew where I stood with Angela and the memories of Graham and my brother. Still, I felt there was a new world out here. One in which my grief could be resolved and I could navigate the hemispheres of my own brain clearly so both sides could work together. Not that I could have put it in so many words.

He was dressed in simple garb: muted tones of soft greens, alpaca browns and duck-down grey. Camouflaged as such, he almost dissolved into the landscape. Although I was able to get a proper look at him this time, his appearance didn't give much away. The expression he wore appeared both solemn and ecstatic. He stared directly at and through me.

'Wearyall Hill is the setting of the *Fisher King* – the Wasteland. A fish effigy etched into its contours represents his castle. Only once its many rooms are filled with soft candlelight, may one step from its defenses and begin to live.'

Since our last meeting, I had met the challenge of moving on. I wanted to get to the same place Graham was at, with all my thoughts and actions flowing in one direction; jettisoning all I did not need, and leaving my comfortable castle.

I heard a voice beside me as I walked.

'Let me tell you of the Moon goddess Arianrhod. Commonly thought of as Welsh, she can also be identified with the Greek goddess Ariadne, whose golden yarn guided her lover through the Minotaur's labyrinth.

'Arian means 'silver' and Rhod means 'wheel' or 'disc.' Her Silver Wheel descends from the stars into the sea. She rules the magical northern realm of Caer Sidi or 'the revolving castle'. Caer Arianrhod, her palace, is the circumpolar stars or the Corona Borealis – the constellation of stars moving around the apparently motionless North Star to which souls withdraw between incarnations.

'Arianrhod is associated with Owl, the Birch tree and Wolf or death, new beginnings and the power of the moon. It is said that through her great Owl-eyes she can see into the darkness of the human subconscious and that she holds magical correspondences with past life difficulties.'

Her story, told in the *Mabinogion*, is one of deception and the disempowerment of women by a patriarchal society. However, Arianrhod – an independent woman – had no intention of practising a chaste virginity.

'The magician King Math, Arianrhod's uncle, was required to keep his feet in the lap of a virgin when not actively engaged in battle. When the post became empty, Gwydion, Arianrhod's brother, was sent out for Caer Sidi to offer the position to her.

'On her arrival at King Math's castle, proof of her virginity was required, by stepping across a magical rod. Consequently, she gave birth to twin boys. The first was called Dylan ail Don, and like a merman he fled to the sea and swam away. The second, a blob-like entity who became Lleu Llaw Gyffes, was scooped up and raised by Gwydion in a magical forest. Fuming from her humiliation at Math's court, Arianrhod laid three curses on the child – she denied the boy a name or the right to bear arms. 'The boy shall have no wife of the race that is now on the Earth.' Each of the curses was broken by trickery, the third by Gwydion who created a woman of flowers, Blodeuwedd, to be his son's wife.

'Arianrhod was defeated and betrayed. She spent the rest of her days at Caer Arianrhod until the sea reclaimed the land, her realm drowned and an epoch ended.'

The storyteller spoke softly. 'You have sought knowledge of past lives and your ancestors. Now, Arianrhod speaks to you, requiring you delve into your soul – release the past and allow rebirth and renewal to occur. Be aware of the moon and her fluid changes. Open your heart to the infinite possibilities of the stars. Be like King Arthur's knights and the dead who reside in Caer Arianrhod, seek truth of self.'

I thought of Graham in the Corona Borealis.

He continued. 'Be like Ariadne. When Theseus, her lover, left her, fate had other plans. Gazing after his departing ship, the god Dionysus approached. It was he who secured Ariadne's immortality, making her a constellation in the heavens – in the image of a crown – his wedding gift to her.

'Life may lead us to unpredictable places. Your own heart may be true, but the wheel of fate means that of others may prove unknowable. Husbands, lovers, children – relationships can be rent apart. The smallest detail can be the one that proves most telling. Theseus's own father died as he sailed from Crete, simply because he forgot to change his sail from black to white, and people thought him dead.'

I placed my calluses against my thumbs. I was in the mood to cast a sail – black as pitch or white as milk – I wasn't in a mood for half measures.

'You have an epic journey ahead of you. One that requires you to feel the potential end before you re-visit the beginning. Death, even of a part of your identity, will produce a sudden vacuum – a loss of attachment that will require grief to heal.'

One can't always be sure one has an eternal spot in the stars to return to. Isn't that the whole point of setting out on an adventure? You weigh up your current life and try it against another. Sometimes you return empty-handed. Other times you learn that you've lost nothing anyway. As with Ariadne, though, that kind of realization only comes later. The weaver had to lose her lover to secure that spot in the sky. Look at me now. I started this day enveloped in grief and hours later, have no desire to return home for the evening. How exhilarating to have Welsh and Greek myth to relive, while walking in the Somersetshire hills. Everyone should be so lucky.

'Anymore?' I wanted to ask. But it didn't do to jog the storyteller into action. One moved at the speed of his breath. Like stepping into a pool, the first shallow steps were always the most tentative and warm.

The hill was steep and furrowed like the gills of a large fish. Underfoot, brown couch grass and sparse vegetation smelt sour and under-nourished. I needed to climb to get away from it. At the same time, a wasteland of sprawling brambles warned of the dangers of throwing oneself upon one's emotions.

My legs were pulling me and my thoughts in one direction – away from the old Graham and my home. I wanted to keep walking till the Corona Borealis was visible above us. And if I got lost? Well, I was ingenious. I could weave a thread.

Then a strange toning – *Aum, Aum, Aum* – arose, entering me directly, soothing me. In a singsong tone, the storyteller confided, 'Our aim is to free the sinuous movement of subtle energy up and down the spine. No more checking of movements and impulses. To experience, at will, a communion between mind and body. This requires the conception of a new idea which will need to be mothered.'

That word. It did not sound so out of keeping up here on the hill. Fallen upon my own resources, but not yet free from old baggage, I felt capable of a fierce maternity.

'The Irish sea-god Manannán guards the gateway to deeper levels of consciousness. Janus-like, he looks simultaneously inwards and outwards, protecting us from energies we are not able – or willing – to bear. To pass beyond him is to court death. Those able to lift the veil can dissolve the influence of the planets and even their astrological birth pattern, allowing entry to the secrets of spiritual enlightenment.'

So there more were gatekeepers. Bring them on.

The land was crowned by a small copse of trees spilling down the hill, and a lone hawthorn adorned with faded ribbons. From somewhere deep down, I recalled the earliest of all poems – *The Epic of Gilgamesh* – and the hawthorn tree which is a gateway to fairyland.

Sweaty and tired, we reached the top of the peninsular and an ancient entry-point to the mystical Isle of Avalon. The Tor loomed in the near distance and the sea moors flowed below us.

As he touched the trunk of the holy thorn, the old storyteller spoke. 'Protect our hearts, resolve our grief and help us to let go of the past. We acknowledge that trees are masters of stillness and understand the natural cycles of growth and decay. They recognize that breaking down is as important as growth.'

He stood there, silently, for what seemed to be an eternity, then he directed me. 'Now you must do the same.'

In the early hours of the following day, I passed Graham's old house and drove out over the water-logged sea moors – eerily lit by the full moon in Cancer, a moon which brings us back home, to the family, to the origin story.

It was still dark when I passed through Aller, where Alfred burned his cakes, and through the Zoylands, where Polish refugees were once housed. I arrived at the coast as dawn was breaking over the swirling waters. Grey and ominous, it was blowing a gale. After casting a circle, I tossed the healing bundle into the great tidal waters of the Severn Estuary.

'It is done!'

At that moment, the winds calmed, the heavy skies lifted, and the sun peaked from a golden aureole to bring the new day.

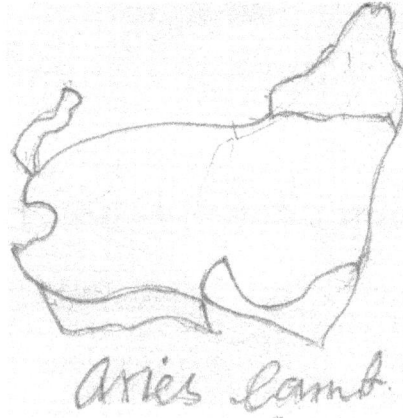

aries lamb

Aries, March 21st – April 20th

Aries represents new life and the will to manifest the self. It is the embodiment of self as a being.

Aries is associated with the planet Mars and the first house. Mars shows the way we initiate new projects and the way we project ourselves – physically, emotionally and mentally. The first house represents birth along with our personality, health and physical appearance. It is the house where we want to move on.

Associated places: Walton Hill, Walton, Street, Street Church

Chapter Ten – Walton Hill

Dawn broke, a profusion of red, ochre, passion fruit and bright orange. Birdsong sounded like the whole of creation was joining in. It was to be breakfast on the lamb's feet looking out over bright ribbons of pink down on the Somerset droves.

On the Glastonbury zodiac effigy, the lamb's feet are tucked under its body, knees facing east, trotters west. Only two trotters are visible. One is on Walton Hill, whilst the other houses a youth hostel. Off to the north, on the lamb's neck is the town of Street. Feet represent our understanding – of ourselves, of life, of others. The lamb is typically a sacrificial animal and symbolizes innocence and purity.

Crossing the wide grassy verge beyond the hostel nestled in the tree line, we headed down a woodland path. Protected from the busy road, the fauna and flora were healthy and abundant – dragonflies darted, blackbirds and thrushes chattered noisily and the scent of newly born fox cubs and rustle of young badgers making their first visit to the outside world, was discernible.

The old man's hawthorn stick thudded rhythmically. Bending low, he picked downy primrose leaves and dark green, heart-shaped violet leaves, along with wild chives and ramsons, to add to our meal. New shoots and succulent leaves of young wood sorrel and jack-by-the-hedge were emerging, with their oxalic acid and garlic-mustard flavour.

Our camp set up, the storyteller busied himself drawing a starling and a murmuration across the wetlands, the collar of his sheepskin coat pulled up against the breeze. He planted his faded crimson running shoes in the dewy grasses wearing a vivid red, cloth cap, his concentration intense and head cocked – almost upside down. 'It is easier this way. To draw upside-down, like a tree sees things.

'The starling teaches us the correct etiquette in a group setting. How to behave in our community with friends and family. She tells us when it is time to speak up, to have a voice. What messages do the starlings and this landscape of new beginnings have to tell you?'

I was preoccupied. Angela's anger and confusion about the antics of powerful people was running through my head. She recounted the same endless story without ever finding a solution. Her mind seemed as though it might burst. Eventually, we always laughed together, she with her wine glass stem clutched like a cigarette between her fingers. But it was like clinking glasses with a headstone. Dark laughter.

Rhythmic breathing slowed my inner chatter – a deep breath in and then out again, to a four beat. After a few minutes he spoke again. 'We need to find your core belief – the story you have re-enacted time and again. This theme will end up being your life purpose and the reason why you have reincarnated. Let your feet grow roots into the centre of the earth. Imagine a star high above your head. Connect inwards and upwards, then lie prostrate on the ground facing south. Gifts may be found from the Gods or you may need to leave something behind.'

As I lay there, the answer came. It is true that stories indoctrinated into a person before the age of seven have life-lasting effects. Mine was connected to my childhood illness. A child's world in which the angry words of a village doctor, his dictate, took me from my first tentative steps to an incarceration lasting two years. Those stakes had never been forgotten.

Later, well breakfasted, lying on the grass below the windmill on Walton Hill, I watched the skies change as I listened.

'There was once an ideal knight, Sir Gawain, a nephew of King Arthur. Like all the knights of the Round Table he followed a code of chivalry, remaining faithful to his word. That was until his baptism with the mysterious Green Knight.

'One cold winter's day, King Arthur greeted a stranger holding a bough of holly in his hand. 'Sir, you are welcome here, dismount from your horse and join us for dinner.'

'The Green Knight's eyes flashed. 'My errand is not to sit at ease in your mighty castle. I have come to you in peace, not spoiling for a battle – merely to propose a festive game. One stroke for another, my bared neck on the block and this fine axe as a reward.'

'Does any knight here dare take up my challenge? All I ask is that in a twelvemonth and a day, I will honour my right to repay them in kind.' With his green eyebrows twitching in anticipation he waited for a knight to take him at his word. 'Can this be King Arthur's court? Has the mighty Round Table been overwhelmed?'

'One by one, Arthur's bravest knights drew near, saying, 'What a strange request! Give me your axe and I will gladly grant your wish.' Even Arthur himself took hold of the axe. The stranger stood still and stroked his beard. Then Gawain, sat at Guinevere's side, said, 'I beseech you lord, let this challenge be mine. I am the weakest and my life would be least missed in this foolish affair. Let the king step down and let Sir Gawain enter the game.'

'The Green Knight got himself into position – head bent forward, long locks swept over his crown, his bare neck exposed. Sir Gawain held the axe high and with a hefty swing the sharp blade swept through bone, fat and sinew. Green blood splashed onto the ground as his severed head rolled away.

'To the disbelief of all present, the Green Knight picked up the head then mounted his horse and steadily sat in his saddle. He then turned to the crowd. 'Come to the Green Chapel on New Year's morn as you have sworn to do!' With a jerk of the reins he turned sharply and disappeared.

'After the passage of a year, Gawain set out to fulfil his pledge. The country was wild and the dangers many. Eventually, a splendid castle came into view. Invited in by the Lord, Sir Gawain stayed home with the Lord's Lady as the Lord took himself hunting each day. The knight's stay had one attached condition: at the end of each day the Lord and he were to exchange the gifts they had received.

'On the first two days Gawain accepted only kisses from the seductive
Lady. These he offered up to the Lord, without divulging their
source. In return, the Lord offered braces of pheasant, a deer
and a boar. On the third day, the Lady offered Sir Gawain a gold
ring which beamed like rays of sunlight. The knight refused to
accept it. 'I have nothing to give in return!' he protested. Then
the Lady offered the green sash tied around her waist, enwoven
with charms. 'A mere trifle but something to remember me
by. No man can hurt he who wears it. Hide it from my Lord.'
Sir Gawain, mindful of the approaching encounter with the
Green Knight, accepted her gift. They exchanged three kisses.
At nightfall, the Lord handed over his bag, a fox, while Gawain
offered up the kisses he had received, but no word was said of the
sash below his tunic.

'The day of the challenge arrived. Sir Gawain came across The
Green Knight sharpening his axe in the forest. 'The reckoning of
our wager is upon us,' laughed the Green Knight and he asked Sir
Gawain to expose his bare neck, just as he had done a year prior.
However, each time the axe was set to fall, the Knight moved his
head. 'Look how you flinch in fear! In Arthur's hall my courage
never faltered!' Sir Gawain gathered his nerve. 'You have my
word; I will be steady until your axe has struck.'

'The axe was held aloft. 'May the glory of good King Arthur save
your neck,' spoke the Green Knight and brought the axe down
hard against his opponent's neck. Yet hard as it fell, it barely
broke the skin, leaving merely a slight nick. Sir Gawain exulted.
'You've had your swing!' he told his counterpart. 'Now the
challenge is met.'

'The Green Knight leant on his axe and studied the young man.
'I release you from all further duties. I've had my light-hearted
sport. You kept your promise on the first night, gave me the kiss,
and proved true to your word. You were a little less loyal about
the sash, not for lust but because you loved your life'. Now his
form changed into that of the Lord, and Sir Gawain realized that
the Knight had been testing him. He wept within and was shamed
by the man's gentle words. In an effort to explain himself, he told
the Green Knight, 'I bargained and in so doing abandoned my
kind. Thus, I demonstrated the selflessness and loyalty of a true
knight.'

'At that, the Green Knight bellowed with laughter. 'Your confession has cleansed your sins. Here I give you this gold-embroidered girdle. When you ride amongst rich princes remember your struggle here – the Green Chapel and rich token. Now let us all be friends and feast and be joyful.'

'Beheading, like that of the Green Knight, is a time when severance enters our life – when the hypnotic trance of our conditioning is incised. It may force us to disengage with the cultural mores of the times, those ingrained in institutions like schools, prisons and hospitals. It may represent dismemberment by spirit guides, with the bones put into a boiling cauldron to be cleaned before they are put back together again, and the knight reborn.'

In the ensuing silence, I considered Angela who bore the weight of the world on her shoulders. It was as if a shameful secret lay close to her heart and needed to be hidden away. Sometimes she stood staring into the distance, her face totally blank. I knew I was changing, and this made things harder for her. She was dealing with a moving entity.

Deep down, part of her didn't feel it had a right to exist. She – and I – needed to sever our old stories, our old beliefs, and bring new shoots. While this would leave us exposed, it was a necessary step towards rebirth and new life.

The storyteller shifted his position as if in acknowledgement.

'Like the orb of the Earth, tilting slightly as we enter a natural cycle known as the procession of the equinoxes, our perspective changes as a new Pole star comes into view.

'Really, it is all just a matter of perspective.'

Taurus, April 21st – May 21st

Taurus represents the time in our evolutionary growth of fertility and abundance.

Taurus is associated with the planet Venus and the second house. Venus is associated with the sensations — touch, sight, hearing, taste and smell - which help us build a sense of inner security. The second house reflects our need for both emotional security and support for the physical body. It reflects our personal values and perspectives.

Associated places: Hood Monument, Collard Hill, Tray's Farm, Redlands

Butleigh Monument

Chapter Eleven – Butleigh Monument

My cottage was in chaos, dirty and untidy. The cat flap broken, computer on the blink and the washing machine needing to be replaced. Angela arrived with her concerns and stayed for hours. I didn't need anyone to point out that adrenalin held my body in stasis after her constant chatter. Head overrode heart, or maybe the other way around, and I topped up her drink.

That inky night, a realization came through the silence. I had to find a force, one that released the energies within – found the cracks and set loose the cooling waters beneath. With the light of day, came the first stirrings of new life.

It was Beltane in early May. The great fire festival of the Celts. A time when the veil between the worlds was at its thinnest. An early morning mist lifted to reveal fertile, green fields as I walked through the old forest. Abundance reigned. On the Arthurian map, I was up on the eye of Taurus – where the star Aldebaran sets, and the Pleiades fall. Plants were growing, animals multiplied and birds sang. Scorpius had risen triumphant over Orion.

Butleigh Woods ran in a wide band between a road on one side and a steep incline on the other. Little tracks darted between the glades towards Glastonbury Tor, Dundon hill fort and the Somerset levels.

High above me rose a hundred-foot column containing a spiral staircase with a carved ship at its crown. Once linked to the Hood family home by a mile-long avenue of cedars, the tower represented the energy that runs up the centre of the body when magical forces are aroused.

Much like Irish round towers, or the pyramids, this was a structure built to gather and distribute power. Set on an electromagnetic field, it once had resonance with celestial bodies. In my mind, it stood in isolation, disconnected, able only to observe. Unlike the bountiful woodlands surrounding it, it was trapped like a bull in a byre.

The storyteller stood with his back against an ancient tree. Today, he sported the guise of folk bard – pea-green felt shoes and a matching hat with cocked swan-feather. His ash stick lay on the ground.

'As a tree ages, it becomes wise. Each tree is part of a community which communicates via an underground web of Mycelium, using electrical signals that reach for hundreds of miles. A tree's nervous system is capable of learning and remembering, which expands their neural fields.

'Our bodies can also receive information from the living world and perceive reality in a different way. For most of us, our senses are worn thin by stress and wrong thinking. Yet when they awaken, it is possible to reconnect.'

So he was talking about re-connection – of our constituent parts and to the world outside us.

The old man continued. 'In humans, the central nervous system forms a bridge – between the physical and non-physical – by which complimentary systems such as the endocrine system can be accessed. Rebirth requires the freeing of two dormant serpents of energy, running up and down the spine, and in so doing connects the cortex and limbic system. On reaching the cup-shaped hypothalamus in the head, they secrete fluids which drip onto the base of the pineal gland. Activation of this gland allows a different perspective and contact with the spirit worlds.'

Maybe these were the mysterious electric and magnetic forces the old Priestesses had passed on to kings and important figures in the times of the Druids.

When I turned to face him again, his hand held a flat wooden tile. It was the rune *Isa* – a freezing of event, situation or circumstance.

His voice continued to filter through the birdsong. 'Things are hidden and repressed. You still exist in the knight's nether world, guarded by a giant maiden. Without sleeping with the different aspects of our consciousness there can be no Sun, no life-giving force.

'Today you will go West, to the location of water, to find your cauldron. This is a place of evolutionary forces, growth and pre-historic fertility practices. Here the powers are immense and uncontrollable – they are the vital forces that bring things into existence. Then, we will head East to the place of directed will, determination and potency. These are the qualities of the knight's lance, or Merlin's wand. In the place of the Bard, high mountains stretch down to the Underworld amid big, disruptive elemental forces. Here lies the Well of Mimir – the well of memory or Akashic record.'

His body curled inwards and was still.

'Some parts of the Earth suck in energy and dissolve it whilst others promote evolution. The rocks, minerals, plants and the ghost roads are the earth's physical body.'

Graham had been filled with life-force and evolutive energy. His long limbs swung as he considered Gestalt: 'It's like a magical piece of music which becomes more than the sum of its constituent parts. Something special happens to you inside as you listen.'

And so it was to be for Snow White. She sat patiently by an ancient apple tree, waiting for a dwarf pushing a wheelbarrow full of autumn leaves. He had come before! Where was he?

Sunlight reflected into the leaves above and glistened in the grass. As daylight began to fade, a fiery ribbon of light pointed towards the base of the tree. Snow White peered closer and made out a small, wooden door. In a time within time, she shifted her body into another dimension and entered cautiously. The earth sucked her gently downwards. This day she would enter the world of the dark elves or dwarves — master smiths who could read the stars of the underworld and expertly navigate their dark terrain.

Careful to avoid any dirt or coal dust from the deep mineshaft she fell into, Snow White stood and dusted herself down. Alone and bewildered in this deep forest of her psyche, she did not know which way to turn.

Until that is, she came to a little house. Inside there were seven of everything — plates, glasses, chairs and, upstairs, beds. Suddenly fatigued, she fell asleep. As daylight faded, the dwarf owners returned from their day digging for ore in the mountains. However, the last two were absent, trapped in a huge landslide, unable to move or orientate themselves.

From a warm bed she heard pleading voices sing out. 'Help us please, oh beauty with the snow-white skin, blood red lips and hair the colour of ebony.'

But Snow-White journeyed onwards. The hot, dry dust of a Bedouin desert enveloped her and tall men in red and white-checked head-dresses filed past. They led her ever on.

An invisible door of luminescent oily greens and blues invited her in. Here she experienced the times of Hannibal and his elephant kingdom — warriors and huntsmen plodding over treacherous mountains to conquer new territory. There was blood on their hands and in the memory of those lumbering beasts.

Meanwhile, her stepmother the queen consulted a glass mirror. 'Snow White is fairest now,' it revealed to her.

The queen came far into the forest to offer Snow White a poisoned comb.

Snow White's reverie changed. Deep in her dream world, she combed her luxuriant black locks. Life began to look different. In a beautiful, Arabian gold and white pavilion, adorned with delicate filigree and full of joyous dancing and feasting, a new perspective emerged. At her feet lay piles of split-ends and damaged hair.

The Queen was not one to be thwarted. Trembling with foam and jealousy, she injected an apple with a deep and subtle poison.

Snow White shifted uncomfortably on the bed. Her vision clouded. Once more she was lost in the forest, distracted and without purpose as she tried to find her way out. First, she smelled the sweetness of the apple, then she touched its smooth skin and saw its perfect roundness. Finally, she heard the murmur of its emotions. 'I will cleanse you of all negative thoughts.' She stretched out her hand and took the poisoned fruit. Her red lips tasted its juicy flesh.

Within her long sleep, she heard the dwarves weep for three days without ceasing, felt the cold of her glass case upon the ledge of a rock and saw that one of the dwarves always remained by it, watching. Owl came to school her in the ways of other's deception, then Raven talked about magic, and finally she glimpsed a clear future as Dove cooed gently above her. In the skies, the stars twinkled.

By and by, a king's son came riding past with the two missing dwarves and wheelbarrows tied to his horse. He asked to see the glass case with the king's daughter inside. The poison slipped from her system as soon as she was moved. The Prince and Snow White were to be married.

A gold and white filigree pavilion was erected. Seven dwarves dressed in fine waistcoats arrived. Also in attendance were the Queen, a line of Bedouins in red-and-white head-dress, and hundreds of elephant-handlers. In the middle of the festivities, pairs of red-hot iron shoes were bought in with tongs. Each was forced to put them on and to dance until they fell down dead.

The old apple tree bowed low and wild clapping and laughter could be heard across the lands.

The storyteller rose from the forest floor and shook himself vigorously. Gradually his body returned to its normal stance. Had he been speaking through me? Or had these been my thoughts? Snow White represents the Goddess, I realized. The feminine, right side of the brain which I had cut off.

Through the Goddess, I was able to get back in touch with my senses, reconnect with the seven dwarves – touch, movement, smell, taste, sight, hearing, balance – and feel the wind on my skin as I walked.

The storyteller spoke to me. 'Often, we return to childhood stories to help us unravel events. It is a kind of play-therapy.' My life-force or potency had been stifled to counter the childhood injections. The long years off my feet also took their toll. It was my body's way of protecting me in the short term – a typical trauma reaction whose influence could still be felt.

Angela also had difficulty with her feelings. In the cottage, she would often retreat deep inside herself, leaving me wondering what I had said. Her long hesitant pauses were often so pronounced that I felt compelled to complete her sentences just to get some air back in the room. Yet here was her conundrum: afraid to make decisions on her own she would involve others, only to feel confused and invaded as her ideas began to mimic those around her. Angela was a woman who operated best alone, even though she desperately needed to connect with others.

Once again, the man in the hat was speaking.

'In times of change, like dwarves we can work with the secrets of the inner earth, our subconscious.

'Then our reality alters. Our senses light up. Eventually, like the trees, we may experience a Gestalt, perceiving in the pattern-based way exhibited by nature.'

gemini

Gemini, May 22nd – June 22nd

Gemini represents the duality of the personality and the ability to choose between good and evil. It symbolises the conflict between contradictory thoughts.

Gemini is associated with the planet Mercury and the third house. Mercury symbolizes flow, new beginnings and change. It collects and passes information within the confines of the body's nervous system and with the outside world through communication. The third house reflects the ability to communicate. How we relate our feelings to others. It is the house where something takes place.

Associated places: Castle Brook, Dundon Beacon, Emblett Lane, Lollover Hill, Lugshorn

Compton Dundon
Yew Tree.

Chapter Twelve – Compton Dundon, Yew

A litter of herbs for the spleen and to aid my digestion – nettle, verbena, artichoke and elecampane. Fridge and cupboards exorcised. No wheat, dairy or sugar. I fasted and took myself on retreat to detach myself from all I had known before.

In those dark hours before dawn, Mimi's fur felt silken beneath my palms. I saw her pure-white socks, the dainty ruff around her neck; that permanent lick of cream above her lip. I dreamed she nuzzled up to a dog she normally hated – there in every room I entered at the party held in my honour.

Her touch under my fingers made me realise I was to meet the old storyteller again.

I later found myself at Compton Dundon church beneath its ancient yew tree. 'The yew aids discrimination, helps the immune system and increases energy.' After a short walk through the quaint village, we climbed the steep woodland track towards grassland and a brake of trees. Once at the stile, we were greeted by two miniature ponies looking for titbits.

Apart from the slight breeze on my face and hands, the tumulus at Dundon Hill fort was motionless. I was sitting on the figure's crown, its pineal gland and seat of inspiration and intuition. Liver moor lay below us, at his knee. Up here, the presence of ancestors and faeries seeped into the bones. It was a place of rare magic.

A meadow undulated gradually down to a wooded copse with an old dew pond, the effigy's eye to the left. In the village, a willow grove forms the figure's beating heart. Beyond it lies the site of a group of old standing stones and Orion's Belt.

'In our native mythology, Orion depicts a being of gigantic proportions and potency like the Irish Dagda, the Wayland Smithy and other older fire- and metal-working gods. Christianity's equivalent is the Three Wise Men.'

Well, I knew a little about Orion's Belt. How it broadcast light and frequencies to our world. Rigel, blue-white just below the belt, was a star-forming region housing thousands of nascent stars.

That day, the storyteller was dressed in torn yellow trousers but a neat red vest, like a court jester. One half was disheveled whilst the other shone with the cleanliness of a new beginning. In his hand he held a staff of apple-wood.

'The star sign of your birth, Gemini, represents the twins or opposing opposites. Good and evil, if you like – Castor and Pollux; Cain and Abel.'

It is a strange feeling to be echoing someone else's vibration – feeling for another without wishing to, without even realizing that is what you are doing. There may be hidden fears too – struggles with love relationships, a lack of trust, modeling the dysfunctional other – and an undercurrent of resentment. On and on it goes until, with luck, you see the other for its true self. When that happens, it is possible to retain your own identity and integrity whilst merging with another. A foot in this world and one in another.

My thoughts turned to Angela. To be fair, she had been changing for a while now – more relaxed, less involved in other people's issues. Laughter caught me unawares, for the first time since Graham had left. It was as if his spirit had spoken. Somehow, I knew the old Angela wouldn't be coming back to my cottage.

'The Glastonbury effigy of Gemini has two figures. The one on Dundon Hill is a baby or Christ child; the one at Lugshorn is a griffon, possessing the face, beak, talons and wings of an eagle and the body of a lion. Like Parzival, the griffon is master of astral workings and a guardian of the Soul and Life-essence. It keeps hidden treasures in its nest, alongside its young.'

His voice continued in my inner ear.

'On a bright morning, Queen Guinevere called together ten of her ladies and ten Knights of the Round Table to go 'Maying' in the woods and fields around Westminster. 'Dress in green and bear only light arms!'

'Meliangrance, an evil knight, had got wind of their plans and saw his chance. He desired Guinevere will all his heart, yet feared her consort, Sir Lancelot. Mustering twenty men-at-arms and a hundred archers, Meliagrance set off to abduct the queen. Adorned with flowers, herbs and leaves, as was the ancient custom, Guinevere was caught completely unawares.

'The knights would defend their queen to the death and soon six of the royal company had been badly wounded as the others fought bravely on.

'Lay down your arms!' commanded Queen Guinevere, and with that opened negotiations with Meliagrance. It was agreed that the 'May' party could stay together on the condition that they forbore contacting Sir Lancelot and did not try to escape. However, the queen was sly. A young servant riding her swiftest horse slipped from the scene without detection.

'Sir Lancelot was enraged to hear of this abduction. Calling for armour and weapons, he and his consort, the loyal Sir Lavaine, galloped towards Meliagrance's castle. Meliagrance lived on a perfectly square island. The only access to the mainland was over a narrow causeway, via The Sword Bridge. At each corner stood a palace with crystal walls and in the centre a fountain gurgled up through a gilded copper horn. Many men were beheaded there.

'Sir Lancelot and Sir Lavaine crossed Westminster Bridge, broached the Thames at Lambeth and braved the arrows which claimed the life of Sir Lancelot's horse. 'Sir Meliagrance!' called the vengeful knight, 'Traitor of the Round Table! I challenge you to a battle to the death!'

'That evening, against Sir Lavaine's advice, Sir Lancelot mounted a ladder and climbed up to Queen Guinevere's chamber. Wrenching free the window's iron bars, he cut his hand in the process. At sunrise he climbed back through the window.

'There is blood on your sheets! You have been lying with one of your wounded knights,' hissed Meliagrance. Although the queen pleaded her innocence, Meliagrance was steadfast in his rage. 'King Arthur shall be informed and if found guilty, you will be burnt at the stake.'

'Sir Lancelot proposed a duel conducted before King Arthur and Camelot, to determine the Queen's innocence. Should Sir Meliagrance win, the Queen's guilt would be established. Should the day belong to Sir Lancelot, then Guinevere's innocence would be manifest.

'King Arthur was reluctant to put his Queen on trial but he had to uphold the laws of the land. A trial by combat was agreed. However, Sir Lancelot could not be found. Secretly imprisoned in Sir Meliagrance's castle, he was being gradually seduced by a waiting lady. 'All I want is a single kiss,' she would say. Days passed before Lancelot conceded. Yet with this action his armour and weapons magically appeared. Mounted on a white charger he made for Westminster and mortal combat with Sir Meliagrance.

'Guinevere had been tied to the stake ready to be burnt yet still her champion would not come. In his absence, Sir Lavaine was ready to stand in and do battle for the Queen. As he readied himself for combat, Sir Lancelot appeared. With the queen's honour at stake, the two knights fell to. Yet after one crushing blow, Sir Meliagrance hit the ground and refused to resume battle. 'Spare me!' he begged and could not be persuaded to stand up again. Now, new conditions were set. Lancelot was to fight bare-headed, with no armour on the left side of his body and with his left hand tied behind his back. With only a sword in his right hand the battle recommenced. Lancelot was deft and strong. With a powerful blow to Meliagrance's head, he killed him outright.

'Guinevere is innocent!' Lancelot declared as he, Guinevere and Arthur embraced.

'Like Arthur, you have also experienced the dissipation of part of your nature. You were young yourself when a rogue knight took mastery of your brain, and led to your feelings being subdued. All your symptoms – the re-enactments and disappearing acts, the inertia and numbness – are a biological response beyond your control. You need to release the reprobate energy that has been trapped in your body and nervous system since you were a small child.

'If Sir Lancelot is our heart and King Arthur our mind, spirit or higher self, then Queen Guinevere is the messenger. When she gets abducted we cannot speak our truth or connect well with others.'

Placing his hands gently on my head, the old man murmured, 'We haven't been able to do this all at once. Otherwise your psyche, like Arthur's round table, may have fractured, and the structure not held. To shift your feeling-awareness into your body, engage with your navel, attend the areas of comfort and discomfort. What are they telling you? Gently encourage your body, the chemical processes in the cells, back into a state of health.'

An unfamiliar energy coursed through me, each part tingling until both my face and hips became hot to the touch.

I soon became conscious of a pony nuzzling my thigh, its nose foraging for treats around my pocket. As my eyes opened, an image of Glastonbury Tor appeared through a hole in the tree line. Damp grass stuck to my splayed fingers and an insect crawled over my hand.

'If you can fully open the feeling centres down your body, front and back, eventually you may see inside, like an X-ray machine. Then you might detect the health of a pineal gland or feel an organ such as the liver. See, hear and feel the symphony around you.

'Just notice and be with the feelings in your body.'

Over time, my body let go. The childhood numbness which had enveloped me in times of hurt and grief, began to soften, became more allowing and fluid. Each of the many re-enactments during my life made sense of that never-ending circle of dramas. My body and mind benefited from the creativity of those who acted out a role – family, friends, work colleagues and strangers – a cast who willingly helped me relive the experiences which had overwhelmed me.

I began to see the weave of my life, to trust in the universe.

One night, my body shook uncontrollably, a typical trauma-release mechanism. I sensed the storyteller.

Cancer, June 23rd – July 23rd

Cancer is where we digest our experiences. It is symbolized by a Crab with its hard shell, soft interior and tenacious emotional grip.

Cancer is associated with the Moon and the fourth house. The Moon represents the feminine principle — the mother and all females — which nurtures a seed and brings it to maturity. It is the activator of the masculine Ego. The fourth house reflects the home environment and has strong associations with what has been inherited — genes or property. It represents peace, romance, mysticism and the final outcome.

Associated places: Red Lake, Liver Moor, River Cary

Liver Moor

Chapter Thirteen – Liver Moor

Cancer, the ship on the sea moors was the place to learn how to digest experiences, handle crises and grow emotionally. Sat under an old, gnarled willow somewhere between the ancient capital of Wessex, now Somerton, and the village of Compton Dundon, we watched as the mists parted to reveal a slow-moving stream meandering down to the Severn Estuary.

That last day, the storyteller was dressed simply, in faded blue jeans and a white T-shirt. Around his waist he wore a multi-coloured belt and he wore brown leather sandals on his feet. 'This crisscross network of waterways drains all the sea moor. The same canals were dug by mediaeval monks to divert the Brue's floodwaters from Glastonbury. Imagine you are sitting in the timbers of an old ship's hull, its width and length encompassing the Liver Moor.'

The choppy willow trees and air currents billowed past as we sat ensconced in the ancient ship. Its great hull was marked out by hundreds of green fields, each defined by an ancient drainage ditch, a rhyne, at its edges. Along the inner side of the ship's steering mechanism meandered the river Cary, slow and steady. Above us, Dundon fort resembled a small child cradled between two giant masts. The watery ground rocked and swayed gently as if we were sailing with a following wind. Everything seemed fluid and mobile.

'The willow is ours,' the storyteller said, looking up. 'Somerset's own symbol of nature, fertility and life. It can withstand the greatest challenges. Remember that when the narrative of our life is meaningful we are happier and more able to metabolise any adversity that comes our way. '

Childhood illness and bereavement had taken me to the edges of insanity – like a shamanic trance or schizophrenic vision. Now, I realised that they were mysterious gifts, forcing me to awaken to the true nature of the world, one beyond the social constructs of our times. Gifts taking me on a journey into the archetypes of the collective unconscious, into the Underworld.

I thought of myself sat in the chair where Angela drank her gins and tonic. Where Graham sat in a quiet stillness, as if part of him had dropped down to feel the impulses within. Each of us set on our paths. Some requiring centuries of re-calibration.

The teller was busy with a pencil. 'Out here, on a dark, clear night you can see the stars of Lepus – the Hare – fall on the boat. Be warned, it is fleet of foot and a challenge to catch.'

When he next turned to me, it was to share a picture of boxing hares.

'Young hares are so well-developed that they can fend for themselves within a few hours of birth. And yet they have their own dependencies. Without an abundance of snowy owl, the snowshoe hare will fall into decline. Nothing walks the rim alone.'

By now, I understood how our feelings drive our physical reality. We carry our experiences with us – both inside and outside of linear time. Not just part of the pattern, we are the pattern. All experience is instantaneously interconnected. I also saw how being consciously aware of my body would make physical experience more intense, allowing me to interpret any setting or terrain and to shape myself accordingly.

His voice continued. 'With your new awareness, once you embrace different realities – ones beyond the constructs of time - there is a choice between contentment or lack and deprivation.' I was reminded of Arianrhod's 'revolving castle' or the Irish sea-god Manannán mac Lir with his 'spinning castle' on the sea bottom.

He paused. 'You must accept your mortality, as the prospect of death is at the root of all your fears. To realise you have been living in a castle which lacks solid foundations – one ruled by a villain. Your boundaries have been invaded and needs are unmet. Many of your emotions – such as pity and terror at another's suffering – have been just a reflection of yourself. The structures of the psyche, or Arthur's Round Table, are common to all mankind.'

With fingers splayed inches from his body, the old storyteller demonstrated. 'Our physical body is covered in different etheric layers. What lies beneath our *skin* is connected with any physical trauma or disease. The *mental-emotional* layer causes us to repeat emotional patterns (*hungry ghosts* or habitual ways of thinking and acting). Whilst, the *etheric* or *soul* layer organises our physical reality and the *spiritual* layer is about our spiritual journey and degree of evolution. The earth's electromagnetic field is the glue that holds them all together.'

But how to manifest or allow change was a different matter! To honour both the ancestors and the Gods. Did I have to practice how to embody light – the colours of the rainbow – or simply learn to get out of my own way?

'Now you have dealt with your repressed childhood memories, there will be a rebirth and other worlds will open. You will return to a new, more vibrant community including many who have been, until now, lost to you: some still within a physical body – family, friends, neighbours - and some without one – the ancestors. As another chapter unfolds, put on the masks of your life roles but take them off at home so you can be in awe and in gratitude. It is important to be creative, to be inspired. Then allow the synchronicities to happen.

'The great king and prophet Merlin endured many hardships. Yet, over time he became mindful of himself and his kindred – he learned about the cycle of the seasons, stellar lore and the creation of worlds.

'Before all of this came to be, the years passed and strife arose between the chiefs of the kingdom. A great battle commenced between Peredur, king of the North Welsh and Gwenddoleu, ruler of the realm of Scotland. Merlin mourned the tragic loss of life, the heroes who died in battle and most of all the three brothers of Peredur. Laid prostrate on the ground he rolled around consumed by grief and would not be comforted.

'For a whole summer, like a wild animal, he hid in the woods. In time, Merlin entered a prophetic madness – the same fervor which had gripped him as a youth when he talked to King Vortigen about the two polarised powers that lay dormant within, a red and a white dragon.

'As winter descended, and with only a wolf as companion, the nuts and fruits became scarce.

'As Merlin bewailed his fate, his lament reached a passer-by and was passed on to a man from the court of Rhydderch, a kingdom ruled by the King of the Cumbrians who was married to Merlin's sister. A messenger was sent to find Merlin, who was sat on top of a mountain surrounded by hazel bushes and thick shrubs. Plucking his cither, the messenger gained the wild man's attention and calmed by the sweet music Merlin's thoughts became clear.

'Merlin returned to the court. Yet unable to abide the crowds of people his madness returned. Restrained by strong chain, he was forcibly made to remain there. One day, he suddenly smiled, leading to his sister setting a test of his sanity. Merlin offered a triple prophesy. In time it came true in a surprising matter – a man hunting a stag fell over a cliff and with one foot caught in a tree drowned in the water below. Merlin was begged and bribed to remain, to hold a royal scepter and rule over a warlike people, but material artefacts no longer tempted him.

The storyteller bent forward to whisper in my ear. 'Society is no longer attuned to the course of the planets or to the mythologies of ancient Britain. In time, as Merlin predicted, it will change again, beyond all things you currently recognise. Soon a rare planetary alignment will push us to learn different rules for our work and life. You will gain a new internal map, a blueprint for living.

'We humans are merely a reflection of the skies above and of our ancestral patterning. A microcosm of the microcosm. Don't get too heady and full of yourself or fight with one arm behind your back. Any powers come from the spirit world, the ancestors, the *Tír fo Thuinn*. Like Arthur, hallow the family hearth and embrace the culture you live in.'

He bid me to come closer and copy him. With hands held up like a boxer, as if he was preparing to fight the Draco for the golden apples in the gardens of the Hesperides, he advised, 'Continue to cultivate the *felt* sense – a doorway into spiritual states. To marry together the two opposing forces: magnetic and electric, moon and sun, past-memories and the life force. This will release the stagnant waters within, those difficulties in your own life and the lives of unwell ancestors.

'Above all, remember that enlightenment is an evolutionary process, one of utmost importance; yet it may not be something you are destined to achieve in this lifetime. Only the weavers of fate, the *Norns*, know your personal web of Wyrd.'

At last, King Arthur's journey made sense to me – his love of Queen Guinevere and need for Sir Lancelot; the importance of rebirth, a second opportunity to regain all that has been lost, and of letting younger knights step forward. I saw what it could mean to be awake, to have potency and feeling in your body and clarity of mind, to achieve the holy grail of intuition. The keys for life to change beyond recognition.

Casually, we sauntered off together as if we were one.

*

Burrow Mump

Sometimes there was a sense of Graham in the cottage, standing in a corner or sitting on the couch. At New Year, it felt as if he was in the car with me as I travelled though Hell's gate and Oath to the gateway of Burrow Mump or the Girt Dog's snout. Once there, the river Tone – its tongue – reconnected us to the moon's gravitational field and tides, the Mother and all females.

He sent messages and gifts – people or things suddenly appeared at important times. Sometimes it was as if a hand gently pushed me from behind. Two small stones, one dusty red and the other dappled, beckoned me to hold them in my hand... only for me to see a larger hand envelope mine. When I walked the landscape, odd places made me feel elated or grief-stricken. It was as if the energy of each location spoke through the soles of my feet. Then, the words of Graham's song came into my head, 'What's the name of the game?' In time, Graham appeared as an orb of light, a fairy presence carrying his essence. Like the Children of Lir's mother, he had come to help.

I began to laugh. The cleverness of it all.

The mysteries of the zodiac and its potential effects on Arthur's round table or our psyche; the need to return to a landscape that embodied my own stories and vibration; the role of Angela whose constrictions broadcast her dramas outwards like a mirror or echo; Graham himself, whose death proved to be a new beginning; whose secret, whose story was similar to my own.

I had entered the zodiac on the day of a swirling tidal bore, and a portal seemed to open. Somewhere downstream, I heard the sound of hounds coming towards me, sensed *Dormath*, the dog of the Faery Lord of Glastonbury Tor at my side. Now a year later, I stood high above the water-logged sea moors and at the zodiac's old confluence of our bodily senses – smell, taste … Up above was Sirius the Dog-Star.

Towards the end, it occurred to me that like the characters of King Arthur's Round Table, the old storyteller had become a part of me. Somehow each of his tales had spoken to everything going on inside of me. I recalled how, in ceremony, he had used rhythm – drum and harp – to move from this world to the next. His voice was a device for reaching the non-human worlds. With my senses lulled, as if by magic, powers came to help.

Now I no longer need him to tell me that my castle – myself, my family, my home – was where I should feel creative and at peace. Or that stories can hold secret information, and landscape, our homes and ancient monuments can do the same. Or even that 'the salmon of knowledge could save mankind from not knowing what he knows.' There was something about walking with him which lent itself to storytelling and listening. The rhythm induces thinking, perhaps. Or trance. There's something that makes one feel invincible. As if, for just these moments, one may escape one's mortal weight, slip the heavy chain.

So that is how it was.

Afterword

After my discharge from hospital at two years old, my mother thought my personality had changed. Indeed, it wasn't until recently that I understood why her observation all those years ago was true. The trauma of my illness and undiagnosed PTSD had altered the wiring in my brain. In a valiant effort to survive the brutal fear and pain, my brain adapted its neural pathways. It blanked out the experience, froze it and cast it away to a nether region.

My problem was, those memories still existed. Not as a story with a beginning, middle and end which had been integrated into my psyche; rather, as isolated fragments and sensations stored in my body. Whenever triggered or overwhelmed, my unbalanced physiology was at leave to drive my actions, choices and sense of self. The brain's reason centre, the frontal lobes, were overwhelmed by the automatic responses of the reptilian brain, the brain stem and hypothalamus and limbic system along with the sensory processing functions of the thalamus and amygdala.

The limbic system or mammalian brain is the 'seat of emotions' and our danger monitor, arbiter of what is important, judge of what is scary or pleasurable and a command-post for coping with the challenges of living. My childhood experiences had set up a pre-programmed escape plan to manage any feelings of fear or abandonment. Inappropriate mirroring led to not being seen by other people, whilst inflexible frontal lobes resulted in becoming a creature of habit who lacked a sense of joy, innovation and wonder. Meanwhile, any threats to my safety or social connections could lead to the dorsal vagal complex (DVC) taking over and a sort of immobilisation or shutting down.

Our body's messenger system, the Vagus nerve (from the Latin 'to wander'), starts at the base of the brain, travels down to the heart, throughout the stomach area and into the intestines. This master nerve balances the sympathetic and para sympathetic branches of the nervous system and harmonises the heart and brain which supports the development of consciousness including compassion, telepathy, empathy and intuition. If damaged or underdeveloped, through trauma or insufficient production of oxytocin (produced through bonding with our caregivers as infants) it can result in anxiety and depression, stress and inflammation not to mention difficulties with the immune system.

My world was experienced with a different nervous system – one focused on suppressing inner chaos. Any stress or over-excitement joined forces with on-going issues concerning constriction and hyper-vigilance to impact my memory, speech and executive brain functions – including my learning and information-processing abilities. My hijacked brain thus led me to dissociation, regular feelings of being overwhelmed, and attempts to flee. These behaviours came side by side with poor self-esteem, feelings of shame and guilt and issues with addiction and intimate relationships. My brain was a fog and on more than one occasion my reputation lay in tatters.

The challenge has been to both understand and to re-wire my brain. Colleagues, among them highly-qualified speech pathologists and psychologists, told me I had 'premorbid word-finding difficulties', a 'complex personality', Obsessive Compulsive Disorder and autistic traits. The same was true for my partner, a social worker who was once awarded a rare commendation from the Probation Office for working with highly dangerous people, but who clearly struggled with his traumatic past. Yet none of the professionals diagnosed unresolved trauma for which ceremony and ritual, rhythm (drumming, chanting, singing, dancing and theatre), breathing exercises, Yoga, Tai Chi and sweat lodges or more mundane activities like walking in nature, smiling and eating certain foods could prove helpful. None told us that shamanic journeying, work with animals (whether Equine Facilitated Learning or stroking a pet) and bodywork (such as cranio-sacral therapy and massage) or neural-re-programing, Eye movement desensitization and reprocessing (EMDR) or the Pesso Boyden method would assist our brains to integrate the experiences.

While the clues to a diagnosis were scant, a breadcrumb trail did exist. Encouraged, I scurried off to do some research and over time my personal journey towards trauma resolution took shape. Now, eight years later, I am left with questions. My long and successful years of client work in the field of vocational rehabilitation have left me appalled at how few fellow professionals are experienced in the symptoms of – and effective treatments for – trauma. Why are so many people left to untangle this mess alone?

There is conspiracy of silence, indifference and over-resistance to the support and improvement of psychological and physiological welfare concerning trauma. It is as if a complicit agreement that the consequences of trauma are the desired outcome of the human condition has somewhere been established. My sincere hope is that the millions of fellow sufferers – those sustaining trauma in childhood, victims of abuse, neglect and torture, war veterans, the list is essentially endless – obtain timely and appropriate help; and that the help of those who have already taken the journey to trauma release and recovery, might be enlisted.

A Note on the Arthurian Legends

The Glastonbury Zodiac appears in Celtic mythology in the tales
of the great bard, Taliesin. In the *Mabinogion* 'Kylhwch and Olwen'
(perhaps the earliest Arthurian tale) is told alongside stories of
Merlin's character which draws on the Welsh prophet and madman
Myrddin Wyllt. Further afield, the Grail story is close in sentiment
to 'Judar and his brother', a tale from the mystic Sufi tradition. In
earlier Sumerian cosmology, Tiamat, their great sea god (or the
zodiac's whale) represented Chaos and spawned monstrous fish-
men, scorpion men, serpents and dogs. In a great battle, Marduk or
Bel vanquished this brood to the underworld, or Avalon, and in so
doing created heaven and hell.

The zodiac is, however, primarily associated with the fictional
Arthurian Legends – King Arthur, the Round Table and the
Quest for the Holy Grail. The Round Table is said to represent
our psyche and the Grail an initiation journey or symbol of inner
transformation. In the Hebrew Kabala, Arthur is an earth-related
wanderer across the skies. When wounded he is taken to the Isle of
Avalon or the Celtic Isle of the Dead where his soul journeys into
the underworld. *The High History of the Holy Grail* and the *Egyptian Book of the
Dead* are counterparts and an initiation into these mysteries of death.

The Arthurian legends are set around the transition from one major
culture or religion to another. Christianity swept through Europe
at the end of the 4th century, dispossessing Britain's indigenous
Goddess culture and its emphasis on the feminine and individual
responsibility. Re-occurring mythological themes such as *cauldrons of
plenty* which bring the dead to life, *enchantment* and *disenchantment* and *the
Grail quest* help carry the mystery traditions forward.

The Arthurian mysteries have also been linked with Greek
mythology. The name Hercules means King Arthur and the stars

of the constellation of Hercules fall upon Sagittarius – Arthur in the Glastonbury zodiac. In his twelve labours, Hercules fights creatures also found in the zodiac – the Nemean Lion, Cerberus, guardian dog of the underworld and the dragon-serpent Ladon which guards the golden apples. The story of Theseus, one of Jason's crew, has mirror elements in the British myth of the Welsh goddess Arianrhod. Links with Norse mythology and 18th century Northern European tales are tenuous, although some parallels exist with the Arthurian legends.

Like other myths and stories, the medieval legend of King Arthur allows the human psyche to locate meaning and order. At its core, is a quest for human evolution – a return of intuition and our true nature. Along with the Glastonbury zodiac and Somerset landscape, it provides necessary initiatory lessons through a symbolic language.

Historical timeline

- Sumerian civilization existed from the 4th millennium BCE to around 2270 BCE

- The 'Epic of Gilgamesh' poem was loosely based on the historical King Gilgamesh, who ruled Sumerian Uruk (modern day Iraq) in 2700 BCE

- Greek mythology was written in a period roughly equivalent to the Bronze Age – 3000 BCE – 1200 BCE

- The Book of the Dead was in use from around 1550 BCE to around 50 BCE.

- Druids were oppressed by the Romans in the 1st century CE.

- Glastonbury Abbey was founded in 712 CE.

- Construction of Wells cathedral began in about 1175 CE.

- Tales in the *Mabinogion* are dated to the late 11th and 12th centuries.

- *The High History of the Holy Grail* was written in the early half of the 13th Century CE. It was a continuation of Chrétien de Troyes' unfinished work *Perceval, or the Knight of the Grail.*

A note on levels of Consciousness

Consciousness is an evolutionary process – one that continues through life and into death, or after we lose our physical body. Most ancient systems present a model of reality based on three levels or layers. However, others suggest it is a seamless spectrum. These three levels include the highest where we are dealing with cosmic and causal forces, and non-duality. This is the realm of the Gods. A second level, which is a world of subtle elements – fire, water, air and earth – is the home of the astral body, the spirits and archetypal energies such as angels. This is the realm of thought, ego and logic. The material world or third level, where we exist, contains living energies such as electricity and magnetism, flesh and bone. These substances act as a bridge to the other two levels.

In Norse mythology, the nine worlds or *Yggdrasil*, the mighty ash tree, represent aspects of both ourselves and communal consciousness. It is a profound model of reality, time and destiny. The worlds relate to different levels of consciousness, each accessed by a system of gateways and portals. Bifrost, a rainbow bridge connects *Asgard* with *Midgard* or Earth. It is guarded by the ever-vigilant God Heimdall and gives access to a pantheon of Gods and Goddesses. *Yggdrasil* was a vehicle for metaphysical travel and the nine realms are held together by the central axis of the tree.

Freya Aswynn has linked each of the nine worlds to a planet in our solar system. *Hel* is Pluto and *Midgard* is Earth, while the realms of *Loselfeim* and *Vanaheim* are ruled by the planets closest to the sun, Venus and Mercury. These two planets represent the *felt sense*, our intuition and connection to spirit. The outer planets – Pluto (transformation and regeneration), Neptune (dissolver of all boundaries), Uranus (breaking down of traditional values, devised by the Capricorn ethic), Saturn (where we look outside of our self for experience and learning), Jupiter (where we build an understanding of the way in which we see our world) and Mars (the sexual and impulsive urge) – represent this incarnation and the experiences we have come to resolve.

Table showing the links between our planets and the Norse realms

Planet	Planet meaning	Realm	Realm purpose
Jupiter	Helps to develop trust, optimism and goodwill in relationship to our experiences, especially those of our early years.	*Muspelheim*	Ultimate end and new beginnings. Evolutive *Ond, Chi* or *Prana*.
Mars	Reveals much about our basic animal nature –our drive, sexuality and aggressive instincts.	*Swartzelheim*	Subconscious mind. Place to deal with sensuality.
Mercury	How we process information. The nerves and brain. Here we receive a whole concept, or gestalt which goes beyond the senses.	*Vanaheim*	Emotional and astral bodies. Garden of Eden.
Neptune	Reappraisal of boundary / reciprocity issues, separation of self from old ways of being and accessing experiences stored as symbols.	*Nifelheim*	Shapes potential into form. Dissolutive *Ond, Chi* or *Prana*.
Pluto	Symbolises absolute truth and is the great revealer of facts reshaped to suit a story.	*Hel*	Collective unconscious or underworld. The dead and ancestor wisdom.
Saturn	Brings meaning and structure to our lives. Its symbolism often addresses themes of death.	*Jotenheim*	Mental bodies. Big, raw disruptive elemental forces.
Uranus	Brings freedom along with electrifying changes. Rules outer space. Where you want to abdicate responsibility and remain untethered.	*Asgard*	Home of the Gods, higher self. An individual's divine spiritual reality.
Venus	Governs the sensations, developed through touch, sight, hearing, taste and smell and is associated with strong feelings of love.	*Loselfeim*	Higher mental bodies. Surrender of your lower self to higher will.

At some point the planets will be aligned for our own death. Then, according to Norse mythology, we move to another level of consciousness, usually *Hel*. For enlightened beings, their consciousness either helps mankind – the altruistic ancestors and angels – or merges with the unknown and their self-image disappears. The realm of *Hel* is different to the Christian concept and a healing place. It rules the reproductive and eliminative processes of life, is associated with intense emotions and sits in the layer of Universal Love.

Once there, we are reborn into another reality, where layers of illusory self-image, down to the cellular level, are stripped away. Then, our thoughts come directly, like a *gestalt* or in a symbol-based fashion, not through the senses. In these realms time flow and causality are at a higher rate of vibration and we can access the 'collective unconscious'. This is the world that Plato, Aristotle, Descartes and Jung, along with numerous mystics and magicians, have accessed and described.

The great mythologist Joseph Campbell states that since the moon landing in the late-1960s, generations have started to view their place in the universe from a different perspective. In the way that Copernicus's a *priori* mathematical judgements about space and time led to a revolution, the moon landing has changed our perception of what is possible. The old mythological bindings have been broken and the scene set to expand human consciousness – a gateway crossed with the old forms dissolving; as yet, however, there is no clear direction forward.

In the meantime, real presence or wholeness in our human or material world necessitates regaining the *felt* sense. Our bodies and their surrounding auras must be cleansed, and old traumas released. Only then may the gateways between different levels of consciousness be found and safely passed through.

Timeline of planetary transits between 2017 and 2020

- *Pluto entered Capricorn in 2008 and will remain there until January 2024. In this astrological sign we are asked to release ourselves from the structures, habits and patterns which have stifled our growth.*

- *Neptune travels through Pisces from February 2012 until early 2025. In this sign we have big plans in mind but often lack the organization and discipline needed to follow through.*

- *Saturn moved into the Capricorn constellation in 2017 where it will remain until December 2020. Both Saturn and Capricorn govern the patriarchy, economy, government and big business, so large transformations can be expected within our institutional structures.*

- The 2017 eclipse in Leo helped us to understand and integrate major life-lessons which will allow unique self-expression to surface. During the eclipse in Cancer, July 2019, we were called to cultivate a deeper understanding of our emotional intelligence needs and what nourishes us.

- Jupiter transited Sagittarius, from November 2018 until early December 2019 bringing good luck and great opportunity.

- Uranus's transit into Taurus, from March 2019 to July 2025, brought a re-evaluation of issues such as finances, abundance, beauty, and earthliness, but through a feminine lens.

- On March 21st, 2019 the supermoon in the first degree of Libra on the Spring Equinox highlighted the need for both independence and togetherness. Whilst the full moon on 19th April 2019 completed the story of conflict and tension between these two needs. It was a time to reappraise old stories and bid farewell to everything that had come to an end.

- August 2019 included two Grand Trines on the 19th and closed with a Grand Trine and stellium in Virgo — the astrological sign associated with the Divine Feminine. This highlighted the task of focusing on one sign, Virgo, and its greater lessons and finished the month, with productivity, along a clear path and a sense of stability.

- The January 12th 2020 conjunction of Pluto, Jupiter and Saturn — the planets of growth and abundance conjoined to the life lesson teacher — has led astrologers to predict a major shift in public consciousness and an entirely new Sociopolitical-Economic Paradigm. It will herald the start of "The Great Transformation" occurring throughout the decade, 2020-2030. A breakthrough to 'another side'.

  This conjunction has only happened twice in the last 2,000 years — 1284 and 1717. The earliest has has been linked to King Philip, falsely accusing all Templars of heresy, leading to their arrest throughout Europe, in 1312, which heralded the dark ages. The conjunction in 1717 has been linked to the Reformation.

A note on Divination

Runes, twenty-four small tiles with ancient symbols on them, are a Norse system of divination, magic and healing. They can be used to access different levels of consciousness in order to diagnose and assist with human situations. Geomancy is a form of divination, often using geographic features, figures or lines to connect to the Earth. Vastu Shastra, Feng Shui and dowsing are all geomantic art forms whilst astrology has its roots in geomancy. These bodies of knowledge evolved to create the most harmonious places and times for human activities. As with the ancients, modern day practitioners sense the energy of a person or place to maximise its potential.

With instruction we can all become diviners – learning to diagnose human auras and locate earth energies and power objects. However, our results will differ. What we feel in our bodies, the sounds we hear and the colours we associate with a person or location are governed by our life experiences and driven by our ability to be 'hollow' and to have cleansed our lives. A good practitioner can see the highest expression of energy in any manifest form – human, animal, mineral and so forth. They are able to recognize the sacred in all things and the relatedness of everything.

At times, stale energy requires clearing – from structures, land, people and businesses. To remove a blockage the practitioner has to connect with the *spirit* or blueprint. First, they acknowledge a form's existing beauty. Then they ask permission for change to occur. Transformation is co-created with the guidance of a higher power.

Often, a diagnostic overview of the form's energy patterns and type is needed. For a building, this might include the underlying Ley lines or watercourses, much like a healer would evaluate a person's aura and any intrusive thought forms and old emotional injuries. Like with people, different earth energy patterns are protective or combative. Some earth locations and structures benefit from the healing attributes of yin water which is said to emit a three-fold pattern or Primary and Secondary halos. Others are based on geopathic stress zones or toxic grid energy including negative Ley energy and underground water. They all have importance and purpose.

Tools are plentiful and up to the individual. They may include shamanic journeying, the divinatory power of a rune or tarot spread or vibrational tools such as rattles, drums, bells and tuning forks along with the more mundane – dowsing pendulums, rods or bobbers, ordnance survey maps and site plans. What the practitioner is trying to locate is the potential for change – where an energetic key is located.

This may be a departed spirit which is trapped, a power spot at the heart of the building or person or a magnetic 'umbilical cord'. Memory can be held in the body, in the land or water, or in an object and it defines and holds the spirit, tone and fabric of that physical form. The human ability to form a relationship with a person, place or object means our mood, patterns of thought and habits of activity can be captured within their essence.

Ceremony and ritual along with high frequencies and magical correspondences will assist with a release. Boundaries need to be drawn, an appropriate time for the work determined and, finally, gifts given as a form of reciprocity. As the energy breaks up, the practitioner must be careful any dislodged energy does not attach itself. This work is not recommended for the faint-hearted or those without established guides in the other worlds.

A note on Ancestral Healing

Ancestral healing is contact with our ancestors – those who are well and not so well – through ritual and ceremony, in order to either revere ancestral gifts or undertake ancestral repair work. This may include identifying ancestral guides, family gifts and burdens, healing the ancestral lines and engaging in psycho pomp (guiding souls to the place of the dead).

The ancestors carry our lineage blessings along with good humour, happiness and health (and possibly creative and artistic talents, intelligence, kindness and intuition). They act as guides and mentors in the spirit worlds to heal any difficult patterns. Families, or individual family members, can also take forward ancestral or intergenerational patterns of pain and abuse. These struggles may include amongst other things: poverty, physical afflictions, addictions, mental illness, physical or emotional abuse and disconnection from the natural world. More difficult patterns need to be lanced and the associated feelings of guilt and shame healed.

Ancestral repair work requires a clear picture of the current state of affairs – sources of spiritual power which feed the lineage and the unwell among the dead. Strong connections may include local landmarks and sacred sites, religious practices, attachments to certain institutions or political affiliations and preferences for leisure and cultural pursuits. In preparation for death, our vitality levels drop, and we begin the process of detaching. Sometimes, if we are in the wrong place, we enter a period of confusion and our diminishing ego seeks to piggyback on another's vitality. The 'unquiet' dead may move into other people's bodies. Spirits can exist in this state of suspended animation for hundreds of years. Or possibly, those who have suffered during their lifetimes, the not yet ancestors, need time and assistance to heal in the afterlife.

It is important for us to connect with the well ancestors, those who lived before the troubled patterns began. Once contact has been established, the relationship can be nourished through genealogy research, personalized practices – ritual and ceremony – and land-based work. As we resolve our ancestral lessons, other family members and people with whom we have a deep connection – departed partners or friends – may also be released. We vibrate on a similar frequency so healing or the dissolution of unhelpful patterns can be initiated by and take place for both those with and without a physical body.

For this work it is important to have no harmonic of fear, which is a middle world emotion. A practitioner needs skills in tracking, merging, image building and to have the power of belief. An essential part of their skill base is the ability to attune – with emotion and vibration – and entrain with a wide range of compassionate allies. This enables them to work with the unquiet dead, possession, problematic other-than human energies, low-vibrational energies, negative thought forms and obsessions, elemental beings, animal spirits and suffering beings. The work enables a family lineage to be restored and groupings of the troubled dead to be woven into the vibrant web of older lineage and ancestral blessings.

Glossaries

Glossary of Animal Meanings

Cat – represents balance between apparent opposites.

Boar – represents abundance, courage and power.

Dove - represents peace of the deepest kind.

Fox – represents discernment and great wisdom.

Hare – represents involvement in a creation story.

Hart (deer) – represents femininity personified.

Hawk – represents messengers from the spirit world.

Horse – represents power, stamina and freedom.

Mole – represents trust in what you feel and psychic impressions.

Owl – represents a deep connection with wisdom, good judgment and knowledge.

Pheasant – represents the law of attraction and knowing when to protect yourself and the people you love.

Raven – represents mystery, divination and an attraction to magical or mystical ways.

Stag – represents the protector of all other animals.

Starling – teaches lessons of group etiquette, social standing and family relations and how one appears to the world in such relationships.

Wolf – a symbol of freedom and wisdom, and a guide on a self-discovery journey.

Glossary of Gods and Goddesses

Apollo – Greek god of the sun, light, music, truth, healing, poetry, and prophesy.

Baldr – Norse god associated with light, beauty, love and happiness. Means "prince".

Minerva – Roman goddess of wisdom, poetry, commerce and medicine.

Manannán mac Lir – Irish sea-god of the Otherworld. A psychopomp (conductor of souls between worlds) with strong associations with the weather and the mists between the worlds.

Odin – Norse god who presided over art, wisdom, war and death.

Glossary of Mythical Images

Apple tree – symbolic of the 'World Tree' whose fruit can represent love, joy and wisdom.

Draco – the Latin word for dragon.

Dragons – symbolic of potent and auspicious powers, particularly control over water, rainfall, typhoon and flood.

Dwarves – symbolize our five senses.

Minotaur – symbolizes the cruelty of man to other beings, men or animals.

Snow White – symbolizes the Goddess.

Glossary of Personal Names

Angela – means angel.

Ariadne – means "most holy".

Arianrhod – derived from the Welsh, meaning "silver wheel" or "round wheel".

Arthur – means noble, courageous.

David – Hebrew name meaning "beloved" or "uncle".

Daedalus – derived from the Greek, meaning "to work cunningly".

Gjöll – Norse giantess who guards the gates of Hel. Means "resounding".

Graham –-means from the great meadow, 'Farm home.'

Guinevere – means fair, white and smooth.

Gawain – means 'May hawk'.

Jason – derived from the Greek, meaning "to heal".

Jean – ultimately derived from the Biblical Hebrew name Yochanan, meaning 'YHWH/The Lord is Gracious'.

Jennifer – derived from the Welsh 'Gwenhwyfar' and old Irish 'Findabair' meaning "the fair one".

Kevin – derived from old Irish Cóemgein, meaning cóem "kind, gentle, handsome" and gein "birth".

Lancelot – means servant.

Mordred – means "controlled, moderated".

Morgan (Le Fey) – means "bright sea, from the shore of the sea".

Parzival – means one who 'pierces the veil'.

Peter – derived from the Greek, meaning "stone or rock".

Phil – derived from the Greek, meaning "friend, dear, beloved".

Theseus – derived from the Greek, meaning "to set, to place".

Vortigern – a title which means 'Great Chief' or 'Supreme Lord'.

Bibliography

Aswynn, F. (1998). *Runes & Feminine Powers. Northern Mysteries & Magic*. Llewellyn Publications.

Brennan, B.A. (1988). *Hands of Light. A Guide to Healing through the Human Energy Field*. Bantam Book.

Brothers Grimm. (1984). *The Complete Illustrated Works of the Brothers Grimm*. Chancellor Press.

Caine, M. (1978). *The Glastonbury Zodiac. Key to the Mysteries of Britain*.

Campbell, J. (1972), *Myths to Live By*. Souvenir Press.

Campbell, J. (2015). *Romance of the Grail. The Magic and Mystery of Arthurian Myth*. New World Library.

Crossley-Holland, K. (1980). *The Penguin book of Norse Myths. Gods of the Vikings*. Penguin Books.

Davies, S. (translator). (2007). *The Mabinogion*. Oxford University Press.

Dieu-Le-Veut, A. (2018). *Stories in the Stars*. The Holistic Works.

Foor, D. (2017). *Ancestral Medicine. Rituals for Personal and Family Healing*. Bear & Company.

Hesse, H. (1922). *Siddhartha*. Penguin Books.

Jacksties, S. (2012). *Somerset Folk Tales*. The History Press.

Jung, C.G. (1961). *Memories, Dreams, Reflections*. Flamingo.

Leitch, Y. (editor). (2013). *Signs & Secrets of the Glastonbury Zodiac*. Avalonian AEON.

MacManaway, B. (1983). *Healing. The Energy that Can Restore Health*. Thorsons Publishers.

Malory, T. (1969) – *Le Morte D'Arthur*. Penguin English Library.

Maltwood, K.E. (1982). *Guide to Glastonbury's Temple of the Stars*. James Clarke Co Ltd.

Maltwood, K.E. (1982). *Enchantments of Britain: or King Arthur's Round Table of the Stars*. James Clarke Co Ltd.

Mehl-Madrona, L. (2007). *Narrative Medicine. The Use of History and Story in the Healing Process*. Bear & Company.

Regardie, I. (1932). *The Art of True Healing. The Unlimited Power of Prayer and Visualisation*. New World Library.

Roberts, A (editor) (1978). *Glastonbury. Ancient Avalon, New Jerusalem.* Rider.

Russell, W. F (1989). *Classic Myths to Read Aloud. The Great Stories of Greek and Roman Mythology.* Three Rivers Press.

Simms, L. (2001). *Our Secret Territory. The Essence of Storytelling.* Sentient Publications.

Scott, M. (1986). *The Children of Lir.* Mammoth.

Sharman-Burke, J and Greene, L. (2009). *The New Mythic Tarot.* Eddison Sadd.

Some, M. P. (1993). *Ritual. Power, Healing and Community.* Swan Raven & Company.

Steinbeck, J. (1976). *The Acts of King Arthur and His Noble Knights.* Penguin Books.

R.J. Stewart, R.J. (2009). *Merlin. The Prophetic Vision and the Mystic Life.* R.J. Stewart Books.

Van der Kolk, B. (2014). *The Body keeps the Score. Mind, Brain and Body in the Transformation of Trauma.* Penguin Books.

Wichland, C. (2011). *Thirty Years Among the Dead.* White Crow Books.

Zheleznova, I. (editor). (2003). *Vasilisa The Beautiful. Russian Fairy Tales.* Fredonia Books.

With Thanks

Thank you to Matt Bryden for his wonderful poetic editing, Blossom Chambers for her layout and my mum for her drawings and illustrations. And to Mark Matousek for his online writing course. Also, to Chrissie Franklin for her professional help and Cal Peacock for her beautiful artwork and promotional support.

Thank you to David Cypher for his friendship and guidance through the Glastonbury zodiac and for his ritual work. To Tim Raven for his kindness, extraordinary healing work and powerful journeys through the runes and Norse world tree. And to Martin Shaw for his myth and story-telling weekends. Also, to Taiga Forest for her ceremonial work and Marjorie and Bond Chapman who guided me through the spirit worlds.

With big thanks to Dr Geoff Rawson for diagnosing my childhood illness, to 'Auntie' Reg Potts for carrying me around and to my brothers Rob, Tim and Oliver, sisters Sue, Gilly and Victoria and cousins as we walked out of this labyrinth together.

Also many thanks to the friends, teachers and therapists for the role they played; Alex Morland, Ali Burnell, Amanda Holden, Ben West, Carol Youngson, Chris Keane, David Kyrell, Della Menday, Emma Finch, Fiona Stewart, Isla Macleod, Geraldine and Gordon Field, Jan Hackett, Julia Pitts, Kristina Pitts, Livvy Adams, Lizzie Booz, Lolly (my cat), Maggie Whaites, Mike Anyan, Nick Welch, Ian Dyke, Marion and Steve Kozlen, Paul Willetts, Roseanne Booth, Rosemary Stibbon, Rosemary Taylor, Ramona Belcher, Ray Ball, Sam Jones, Sharon Coker, Stan Lester, Tim Dunk, Tish Chapman, Tom Jones, Tracey Burke and Trish Boisgard.

Most of all, heartfelt thanks to Kevin Vaughan Jones for his deep love and otherworldly guidance.

Summerlands is the third book in the *Two White Feathers* trilogy

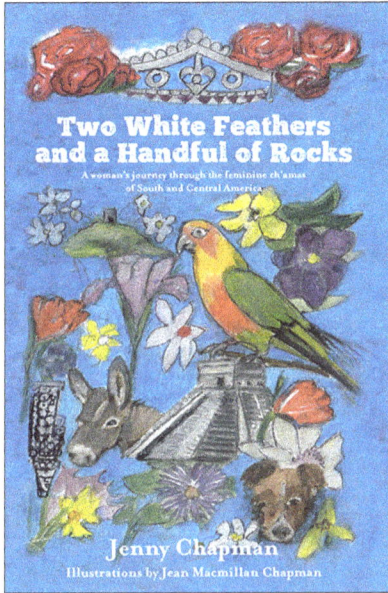

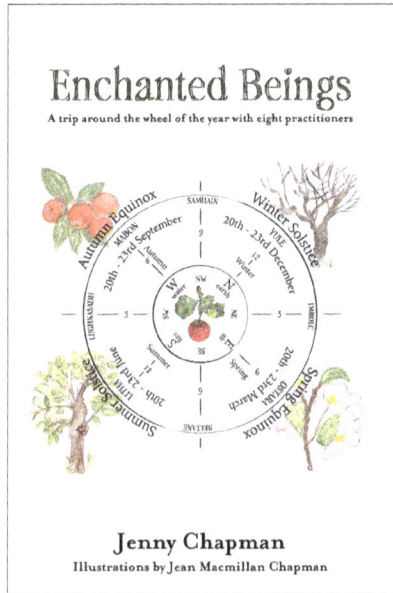

Read as a trilogy, the books describe a journey into the *felt* sense, undertaken over the eight years between 2011 – 2019. It took the author from 'I', through 'We' and onto an understanding of the 'Others'.

For further information please visit.

www.chapmanjenny.com

Author

Jenny was born and raised in Somerton, regularly riding over the sea-moors to Compton Dundon. She was schooled in Street and Glastonbury and her mum has lived in Castle Cary for many years. Each of these locations form part of the giant effigy system known locally as the Glastonbury Zodiac. Throughout her life Jenny has been immersed in story – from an early childhood spent in her mum's playgroup listening to fairy tales, through teenage years avidly reading *The Lord of the Rings* to a passion for books in her adult years.

In her professional life, Jenny has worked with the stories of people who have suffered illness, injury and disability. Over the years, she developed an ability to 'listen' to the underlying *storylines* – the energetic points in a person's story which offer clues to their way of being in the world. Working with the individual, she set up a plan to untangle the key issues – unhelpful behaviours, poor physical or mental health, work they have outgrown and so forth.

Jenny is often called upon to help people in transition with their life path. Those attracted to her work have usually experienced childhood trauma, bereavement or difficulties with the *felt* sense. She is drawn to ceremony, ritual, ancestral work and energy techniques and her practice is centered on places which resonate with an individual – houses, land and sacred places. Along with traditional rehabilitation and case management techniques, her work can include shamanic journeying, energetic transmissions, storytelling and elements of Jungian play therapy.

In her wider community work, Jenny draws on her management and people skills, gained from running a successful Vocational Rehabilitation business and European 'Transfer of Innovation' projects. She is currently a Director for *Paintedhorse*, an equine facilitated learning, Community Interest Company.

www.ingramcontent.com/pod-product-compliance
Lightning Source LLC
Chambersburg PA
CBHW051029030426
42336CB00015B/2783